How to Direct Market Your Beef

By Jan Holder

Handbook Series Book 8
Published by the Sustainable Agriculture Network, Beltsville, MD

Editor/Project Coordinator: Valerie Berton
Design: Design Fish, www.designfish.com
Printing: Jarboe Printing, Washington, D.C.

The book was reviewed by SARE staff as well as Jim Goodman, beef producer, Wonewoc, Wis., A. Lee Meyer, University of Kentucky Extension, Peggy Sechrist, beef producer, Fredericksburg, Texas, and Michael A. Smith, University of Wyoming. Every effort has been made to make this book as accurate as possible and to educate the reader. This text is only a guide, however, and should be used in conjunction with other information sources on direct marketing. The editor, author and publisher disclaim any liability, loss or risk, personal or otherwise, which is incurred as a consequence, directly or indirectly, of the use and application of any of the contents of this book.

This book was published by the Sustainable Agriculture Network (SAN) under cooperative agreements with the Cooperative State Research, Education, and Extension Service, USDA, the University of Maryland and the University of Vermont. SARE works to increase knowledge about – and help farmers and ranchers adopt – practices that are profitable, environmentally sound and good for communities. For more information about SARE grant opportunities, go to www.sare.org. SAN is the national outreach arm of SARE.

To order copies of this book ($14.95 + $5.95 s/h), contact (301) 374-9696, sanpubs@sare.org or www.sare.org/WebStore.

Sustainable Agriculture Network
10300 Baltimore Ave., Bldg. 046
Beltsville, MD 20705-2350
P (301) 504-5236
F (301) 504-5207
san_assoc@sare.org

Library of Congress Cataloging-in-Publication Data
Holder, Jan, 1953 –
How to direct market your beef/by Jan Holder.
    p. cm. – Sustainable Agriculture Network handbook series; bk. 8
ISBN-13: 978-1-888626-11-7

1. Beef – Marketing. 2. Direct marketing. 3. Beef – United States – Marketing. 4. Beef industry – United States. I. Title. II. Series.

HD9433.A2H65 2005
641.3'62'0688 – DC22   2005022003

contents

introduction .... PAGE 1

starting out .... PAGE 5
Find A Niche
Selling the Whole Carcass
How to Cut Up a Carcass
Make $10 Mistakes, Not $1,000 Ones
Stand By Your Price
Expect to Reinvent the Wheel
Frozen vs. Fresh
Organic vs. Natural
Scheduling
Learn How to Cook Your Beef
Processing
Getting a Label
Packaging Your Product
Genetics
Forage

entrepreneurs .... PAGE 44
Carver Family
Hodge Family
Brownlee Family
Elliott/Rude Family
Hatfield Family
James Family
Holder Family

selling product .... PAGE 53
Situational Analysis
Sales Outlets
Distribution and Trucking
Marketing Your Product
Advertising Basics
Public Relations
Record Keeping

growing profit .... PAGE 81
The Future for Small Beef Operations
Developing Growth
Factors that Impact Your Bottom Line

resources .... PAGE 88

PHOTO BY EDWIN REMSBERG

introduction

When my husband and I took over the management of the family ranch in 1992, we thought that it was going to be an idyllic life. We were going to whip the ranch into shape in a few months and then spend the next 20 years canning vegetables and writing the great American novel. We thought that if we just ran things a little more efficiently, the ranch would instantly be profitable.

It took us a couple of years to learn what was really wrong with the ranch. Sure, the place was a little rundown. The houses were in need of repair. The corrals were held together with more baling wire than wood. The land was overgrazed. But we didn't mind hard work, so everything was going to be fine.

Then, slowly, the realization hit us. No matter how hard we worked, no matter what building we repaired or pastures we improved, the ranch was still never going to make it on its own. The beef industry had changed. Just a few generations ago, you could support your family with a herd of 25. Today, with our commodity-based cattle industry, a small cattle rancher was increasingly challenged just to make a living.

After asking around, I found that the only ranchers who were solvent were the ones who had other income. Either the wife or husband worked in town, or in our case, we had a father who was an eye doctor with deep enough pockets to subsidize the ranch. Sure, the really big ranches, the huge ranches, were making it. They could make 3 cents on a carcass and still come out okay. But they were running many thousands of animals. We had a herd of 200. How could we possibly compete?

It was clear that we couldn't. We had to figure out how to sell our beef in a new way. We decided to try to take it from the pasture to the plate without all the middlemen in between. But after contacting an old advertising client in Phoenix who ran a chain of restaurants, I found that we could barely compete with his prices, even after cutting out all those middlemen. So, we decided that we had to make our beef different and better. Then folks would be willing to pay more for it.

To differentiate our product, we thought we could highlight our pesticide-free beef, our range-protection strategies, our "gentle" approach to raising our animals, and our acceptance of predators on the land. After all, we were considered radical, weird and strange for our tree-hugger mentality.

> To differentiate our product, we thought we could highlight our pesticide-free beef, our range-protection strategies, our "gentle" approach to raising our animals, and our acceptance of predators on the land.

Most other cattle ranchers thought that we were nuts. We didn't use pesticides. We treated our cattle as gently as possible. We constantly took classes on ways to use cattle to improve the land. We didn't kill predators. All we had to do was tell people how wonderful we were and they would flock to us in droves and buy our beef! This was going to be so easy. I really couldn't believe that all small producers weren't marketing their own beef.

After reading both of Joel Salatin's books (*Salad Bar Beef* and *Pasture Profits*), we felt that between his ranch-direct program and selling in the nearest local towns, we could market all of our beef. Soon we found that we were too far out in the boonies for ranch-direct selling, the nearest tiny hamlet being 1 ½ hours away. People in the nearest sizeable town 2 ½ hours away weren't going to pay a premium for beef. Many of the residents of those towns seem more impressed with 60-cent-a-pound hamburger than anything that we could come up with. So we decided that we were going to have to sell in Phoenix or Tucson.

We still believed in Joel Salatin's idea of relationship marketing, but realized that our relationships were going to take a slightly different form. Even though people seemed to like the idea of ecologically sensitive ranching, not that many were willing to put their money where their mouths were. Suddenly, what looked like a huge demand turned out to be a few committed people.

We did sell to a local organic buying club (and still do), but to really make it we were going to have to hit the big cities.

Back at the ranch, we asked ourselves, "How are we going to sell beef five and six hours away?" We decided to target stores, restaurants and natural foods distributors.

Years later, it still seems too early to rest on our laurels (is there ever a time when we can rest on our laurels?), but we are very happy with the choices we have made, and sales have gone very well. In 2004, the grass-fed beef industry was estimated to be worth around $5 billion, and growing at a rate of 20 percent per year.

Our Ervin's Grassfed Beef now sells throughout 11 western states through natural food distribution companies, as well as at farmers markets in Arizona. In addition to ground beef, ground beef patties, steaks and roasts, we now also sell pre-cooked marinated roasts and pre-cooked sliced roast beef.

Even though direct selling our beef has increased our bottom line, our company also has helped us to live the life we want, a life on a family ranch.

JAN AND WILL HOLDER ON THEIR ARIZONA RANCH

starting out

Find a Niche

To successfully direct market your beef, you must do something no one else is doing. With conventional beef sales, large companies can produce hamburger for about 60 cents a pound. If you can figure out how to do it for 59 cents a pound and remain profitable, you will be very successful. Obviously we can't do this. So you have to look for other ways of differing yourself from the competition.

Bill Niman, founder of Niman Ranch, is a good example of an entrepreneur finding a niche. He recognized that the products in conventional beef sales varied quite a bit. One day you might get a good steak, another day you won't. (If you are the only game in town, you don't have to care.) All Bill Niman did was offer a consistent product. If you buy a Niman steak, you know it will be good. Hence, you can charge more.

A niche also can be something that is non-tangible. Many of our customers buy our product because we don't kill wolves. That does not make the beef taste any better, but it is a difference that people are willing to pay for. The difference doesn't have to be a real thing, it can also be a perceived thing. For instance, which is better: Coke or Pepsi? They are essentially the same product with different packaging. Remember, if folks can find different niches for sugar water, surely you can find one for beef.

There are lots of these sorts of niches. You just need to be creative to see them. To help you get your juices flowing, here's a list of possible niches:

- Slaughter procedures (for those who want beef slaughtered a certain way)
- Choice-grade grass-fed beef
- Organic
- Corn fed
- Grass fed
- Angus
- Longhorn
- Prime
- Lean
- Guaranteed tender
- From a family farm
- Locally produced
- Humane handling
- Nebraska beef
- Argentina beef
- Ethnic markets

> The emergence of e-coli outbreaks, salmonella, lysteria, mad-cow disease, and hoof-and-mouth disease has opened the door for another marketing opportunity: clean, safe beef.

The emergence of e-coli outbreaks, salmonella, lysteria, mad cow disease, and hoof-and-mouth disease has opened the door for another marketing opportunity: clean, safe beef. Many people are very worried about those problems and are willing to pay more for the peace of mind, knowing the beef they feed their families is safer from contamination. As a small producer, this is one way you can compete and win against the big guys.

The sheer volume of beef and the speed at which they have to process cattle makes it impossible for large producers to provide beef free of contamination. Being small, you have the ability to literally monitor every carcass you sell. You can be much more certain of the safety of your product.

Most niche producers today also are certifying the source of their cattle's feed. This was brought on by concerns that cattle fed rendered animals could cause mad cow disease. It's another way you can differentiate yourself from the pack.

The beef industry needs to make some major structural changes to deal with customer perceptions that beef isn't healthy. Until they do, selling clean, healthy beef is one of the best niche-market opportunities you have as a small producer.

Selling the Whole Carcass

When first starting out to market your own beef, one of the first problems you will face is that it is easy to sell the high-end cuts and hard to sell the low-end cuts.

Restaurants love buying steaks from local ranchers, but steaks only make up about 10 percent of the carcass. You still have a lot of beef to sell.

Conventional beef marketing deals with this problem by using price. That's why chucks, hamburger and rounds are cheap, and loin steaks and tenderloin are expensive, because

everyone wants steaks and tenders. Every day, they have so much beef to sell, and they get on the phone (just like the trading floor of the stock exchange) and sell their beef. Because fresh beef has a limited shelf life, they have to sell it before it spoils. As the industry saying goes, "You have to sell it before you smell it." They just keep going down in price until all their beef is sold.

Marketing on a smaller scale, you can pick your customers and select them in the right proportions to what you need to sell. For example, if a restaurant wants 50 pounds of tenderloin a week, you will have to match that demand with customers who are willing to buy 1,000 pounds of hamburger a week.

> Marketing on a smaller scale, you can pick your customers and select them in the right proportions to what you need to sell.

Of course, you can always sell your other cuts on the conventional market, but you'll have to accept a very low price. Most big meat distributors only deal in huge quantities, which makes it hard for small marketers to "dump" what they can't sell.

You'll also find that the low-end cuts are much more price sensitive than the high-end cuts. You might be able to charge double or triple market price for your tenderloin, but you may have to settle with just 10 to 20 percent more for your ground beef.

Initially, you will probably sell out of steaks and be left with ground beef, limiting your overall sales. People seem ready to pay for a premium steak but balk at $3-a-pound ground beef.

They may not realize there is a difference between yours and the 60-cent-a-pound supermarket version. Once they are hooked on your steak, give them a free pound of ground beef. One pound will usually convince them to buy a balance of all of your cuts.

To make things even more difficult, there are a few cuts in the middle that no one really knows about. People know what a steak is and what hamburger is, but what's a tri tip? What's the difference between a flank and skirt? Being small, you will have a lot of face-to-face interaction with your customers, so you can educate them on how to cook the different cuts.

I've found that with a little planning you can proportion your customers to match how you cut up the carcass and not be forced to sell for a lower price just to get rid of all your beef. You will want to find a lot of hamburger buyers, because about 50 percent of your carcass will be hamburger.

Another way of dealing with the lower demand and lower-priced cuts is to add value to them. The margins on a round roast are not very large, but if you make that round roast into jerky or a ready-to-serve marinated roast, suddenly you've got products that rival the loin steaks in profitability. So if you can't sell it, rather than take a lower price, be creative and think what you could turn it into.

There are also several other parts of the carcass that can become more profitable.

> Another way of dealing with the lower demand and lower-priced cuts is to add value to them. If you make that round roast into jerky or a ready-to-serve marinated roast, suddenly you've got products that rival the loin steaks in profitability.

Your creativity is the only boundary:
- Tongue, livers and kidneys can be mixed with fat, hamburger and vitamins for premium dog food.
- Hides, tendons and "pizzles" can be turned into dog chews.
- Bones can be used for dogs, zoos or wildlife rehabilitation centers.
- Marrow bones are seeing a comeback at high-end restaurants, health food stores and hospitals.
- Ground and dried liver and glands are used as supplements in health food stores.
- Trim can be dried and turned into dog chews.
- Consider these specialties: summer sausage, beef bacon, jerky, deli meats, hot dogs and marinated roasts.

I have had good luck with selling cuts at farmers markets that I can't seem to move elsewhere. Usually, I have had to be a little creative. For instance, I once had a lot of skirt steak that wasn't moving. I added spices, rolled them up, sliced them and labeled them "spiced pinwheel steaks." I sold out in one hour – at $4.50 a pound. These were skirt steaks that we couldn't sell at $1.50 a pound. The secret was that I set up a grill and let people taste samples. I handed out a recipe and cooking instructions for the item with each sale.

At this same farmers market, I sold 32 pounds of flank steak that I had to move. I marinated it in a very simple marinade for an hour

and cut it up and stuck it on skewers. I had 10 people buy the whole skewer for $3 apiece. That comes to about $30 a pound.

However, make sure that you check your local, county and state regulations concerning sampling products and selling value-added products such as spiced pinwheel steaks and marinated cuts. Depending on the laws in your area, they may not be allowed at farmers markets. If you alter a cut after it has been inspected (by adding other ingredients) and labeled, you may void that inspection. Cooking and giving away samples may require you to be inspected and licensed as a restaurant.

How to Cut up a Carcass And How Much You'll Get of Each Cut After You Do

No doubt if you're looking into direct marketing your own beef you've talked to a butcher about how a carcass is cut up, and how much of what cut you can expect from a carcass. If you have and walked away feeling totally mystified, join the club. There are a million ways to cut up a carcass. If that isn't bad enough, different people call the same cuts by different names.

What's the difference between a top sirloin and a T-bone? Or a Kansas City strip steak and a New York strip steak? Or a breakfast steak and a cube steak?

There are a million ways to cut up a carcass. If that isn't bad enough, different people call the same cuts by different names.

I even went in and watched them cut up the carcass, thinking it might help to visualize all this stuff. Actually, it did and I would recommend it highly. Even more, the biggest help to me was a book called *The Beef Buyers Guide.* This is a secret club kind of thing. Everybody in the industry pretends that this is a holy writ, but you won't find it in a bookstore (although you can order it online). This book breaks down the carcass into different pages, tells you all the cuts you can make from a certain section and provides helpful pictures.

For instance, with the rib section you can make a rib steak/bone in/tail on, or rib steak/bone in/tail off, or boneless rib steak, or tied rib roast, and so on. It is a bit of overkill, but it will give you a working knowledge. Plus, it contains the codes that restaurants use, so you'll know when someone calls and says he wants a 1139a (whole tenderloin, ¼-inch trim, lip on).

In actual practice, it turns out no one really knows all of those codes. There are regional differences in what meat people will call the same cut, both in name and in code (a New York strip and a Kansas City strip are the same thing). But if you know them, it will make you look smarter than the conventional meat salesperson.

As I mentioned, you can cut up a carcass many ways. It all depends how much, and of what, you are selling. If you're just starting out and aren't that sure of your quality, start with cull cows. They'll give you excellent hamburger and store-quality tenderloin. The next step up is young cows and steers, which give you tenderloin, stew beef, marinated roasts, jerky and hamburgers. If you're really good, you have the slaughter steer or heifer, which gives you everything.

As a rule of thumb, a 1,000-pound live animal will give you about 300 pounds of saleable beef or, in industry lingo, your "boxed weight." You might hear people talk about getting 50 percent yields (versus your 30 percent). What they are talking about is the "cold carcass" weight, or how much your carcass weighs on the rail. This weight is meaningless; what counts is the weight of the beef you sell. If you are cutting steaks or making hamburger for people, there is a lot of bone you don't get paid for.

Of course, you can divide a carcass into many different cuts (*right*), each of which contributes to your bottom line. Your actual weights may vary 5 percent each way depending upon your genetics and slaughter weight, but this is generally about average.

Make $10, Not $1,000 Mistakes

Once you have decided to market your own beef, it won't take long before you figure out that things would be easier if your marketing effort were bigger. That's because conventional beef marketing is set up to move huge quantities of beef very cheaply. Unfortunately, there are a lot of people who have lost an awful lot of money trying to do this.

Large beef processing and distribution companies can move huge quantities of meat very cheaply because they've been at it awhile. Although we dislike the dominating corporate nature of their business, we have a great deal of respect for what they have been able to accomplish. They do what they do very well.

When we first started out, we made a presentation to a very kind individual with a natural foods distribution company. He informed us that we were not experienced enough or large enough to service them properly. He also suggested that we sell directly to our area's small natural food buying clubs, which were

Tenderloin
12 pounds/carcass
$9.60 per pound
$115.20 gross

New York Strip Steak
14 pounds/carcass
$6.40 per pound
$89.00 gross

Ribeye Steak
24 pounds/carcass
$5.33 per pound
$127.00 gross

Fajita/Stir Fry
6 pounds/carcass
$3.20 per pound
$19.00 gross

Round Roast
67 pounds/carcass
$2.76 per pound
$184.00 gross

Ground Beef
170 pounds/carcass
$1.75 per pound
$297.00 gross

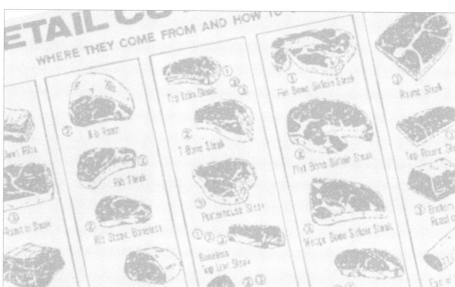

These basic industry definitions help you sound like you know what you're talking about, although you don't really need to know them.

Yield: Percentage of sellable, live beef weight. On average, expect 30 percent. "We're getting a 30-percent yield."

Yield Grade: (Note: Does not actually pertain to yield.) Amount of fat per carcass where 1 is leanest and 5 is the most fatty. Most often applies to the manufacturing of value-added items such as hot dogs and sausages.

Hanging Weight: Weight of carcass on rail following slaughter; somewhat meaningless as carcasses are not sold in this manner.

Cold Carcass Weight (CCW): Weight of carcass on rail following chilling. Grain-fed cattle shrink ± 5% from hanging weight (mostly water loss), while grass-fed cattle have minimal to none.

USDA Grading System: Voluntary, inconsistently used method for grading beef based on age and total marbling. USDA grades include: prime, choice, select, standard, commercial, utility, cutter and canner. Some products carry merchandising or packer house brands. Non-graded cuts are sometimes called "no rolls" since a grade stamp has not been "rolled" onto the carcass.

Wurter Brazelton Sheer Test: Method of testing for tenderness in which seven samples taken from a cooked cut are measured for the force it takes to cut it, then averaged to produce a tenderness score.

his customers. Even though we were a trifle (okay, maybe a lot) peeved at his suggestion, it turned out to be some of the best advice we have gotten.

We learned what cuts the customers want, how they want it packaged, and how many pounds to put in each package — as well as a myriad of other details we hadn't even thought about. For example, we found out that customers liked beef in see-through fresh food packages better than if it was wrapped in butcher paper, because they could see the meat.

Moreover, we found out that our customers like 1-pound packages of ground beef more than 2-pound packages (2 pounds was too much for most families).

If you are just starting out, sell to your friends or to groups. Sell sides of beef using an ad in the local paper. Call up local groups — like the Elks — and ask if you can sell them the beef for their next big barbecue. Invite comments and criticism. You need all these experiences.

If people criticize your beef — rightly or wrongly — the natural thing to do is defend yourself. Try not to. It will only create ill will between you and your customers. Just be gracious and thank them for their comments. Offer their money back.

When first starting out, you will need to restrain yourself from being big. Start small and stay small until you have worked your way through all the surprises. Then take on some more demand. Do it incrementally,

do it slowly. No one gets everything right. There are too many things to go wrong. The mistake that gets you won't be one you know, it'll be one you hadn't even considered. Your margins won't be as big when you are small. By the same token, a mistake won't kill you either. Take it slow, work your way through mistakes, and be creative. There is always more than one way to skin a cat.

Don't buy a refrigerated truck. Don't buy any processing equipment. Don't buy a processing facility. Lease or hire it until you are a few years down the road.

Jim Goodman of Wonewoc, Wis., bought a walk-in freezer as his only initial start-up equipment. He says his business would have been impossible without it. "It allows us to sell on the farm, makes getting ready for the farmers market, where all meat must be sold frozen, quick and easy, with no running to rented freezer sites," he says.

> If you are just starting out, sell to your friends or to groups. Sell sides of beef using an ad in the local paper. Call up local groups – like the Elks – and ask if you can sell them the beef for their next big barbecue.

Stand By Your Price

The easiest way to determine your price is to start with the cow and work your way to the consumer. It costs you x to make a 500-pound calf, x to finish it, x to process it, and x to store, transport, package and distribute it. Once you know all that, you can simply add what you think is a fair profit. You may end up having to revise it, but at least you will know where your break-even point is. The point is to create a price and stick to it. You can count on folks trying to talk you down. Don't take it personally. This is how the commodity game is played. However, don't be afraid to turn some folks down because of price. You can't be all things to all people, and there are plenty of other places a person can find cheap beef.

Items to be worked into your price:
- Cost of creating a saleable animal (labor, supplement, replacement cost, etc.)
- Land
- Finishing
- Transportation to slaughter facility
- Slaughter fee
- Processing
- Packaging
- Storage
- Transportation to retail
- Promotion

If you are still not sure that your prices are in line with what the customer will pay, go to a big natural foods store in the nearest thriving metropolis, and check out the prices. Write down the price of each cut, per pound, and compare them with yours. Figure that the retail price is about 30 percent higher than what the wholesaler sold it for. If they ask what the heck you're doing, you can always say that you are planning a big shindig and are on a tight budget.

One mistake we made early on was not pricing our beef high enough. People didn't perceive this as a bargain. They perceived

The easiest way to determine your price is to start with the cow and work your way to the consumer.

our beef as inferior to beef that sold for a higher price. So we simply priced ourselves higher and made everyone happy.

Refer to *Factors that Impact Your Bottom Line* (p. 84) for more tips on pricing.

Expect to Reinvent the Wheel

Author Allan Nation's view of the learning curve shows the potential downside to being too ambitious without doing your research first. In his version, naive enthusiasm leads to total despair. In other words, take a good look before you leap into marketing your own beef.

As stated earlier, the conventional beef marketing system is not set up to deal with small producers. So even though this country has an excellent infrastructure for transporting, processing, packaging and distributing beef, it means nothing to you. It costs almost as much to ship 100 pounds of beef across town as it does to ship 1 ton across the country. These are frustrating, but important facts. You will need to get used to reinventing the wheel, because, at least in this case, the wheel wasn't designed for you.

Actually it's even harder than that. Not only do you have to reinvent something, but you also are challenging the status quo.

As in all industries, there are good people and bad people. You will probably run into a few of these bad apples along the way.

They'll probably be rude; they might laugh at you, or act condescending and tell you that you will never make it. Try not to take it personally, and don't let their negativity rub off on you.

The majority of folks who try to market their own beef run into a few of these obstacles, get frustrated and quit because "it's impossible." It's not impossible. It might be crazy, it might be work, and it might ruffle someone's feathers. But it's not impossible. What it will be is creative. Just plan on having to customize every little step, from pasture to plate, and take nothing for granted.

Frozen vs. Fresh

There is an age-old debate among meat scientists that asks the question, "Which is better: fresh or frozen?" Our experience has been that there is no difference in quality. In fact, our frozen beef may be more tender because fresh, conventionally marketed beef goes through its aging process during transport. So if you happen to be first on the delivery that week, your beef hasn't aged enough. There is a discoloration of the beef when you freeze it, from a cherry red color when it's fresh, to more of a rose color when it's frozen. After it's cooked, it looks the same as fresh beef.

However, there is a perceived difference. We have yet to meet a chef who will accept a frozen product. We've tried blind taste tests and the whole shebang, but they just

want a fresh product, it's just their deal. There are also some retail customers who feel the same way, but it's even sillier with them. Of course, the first thing they do with the beef when they get home is throw it in the freezer.

Organic vs. Natural

Until the summer of 1999, the USDA would not recognize, nor issue labels, that made any kind of claim to being organic (at least as far as beef was concerned). That's how *natural* beef got started. Legally, the USDA use of *natural* only meant that your beef had no artificial additives and was minimally processed. So unless you injected your sirloin with Red Dye No. 5 or ground it and reformed it into steak nuggets, you could qualify as *natural*.

However, some folks felt they could offer more and strove for an "organic" label. The USDA has since finalized its organic label, including one for beef. As part of that, USDA recognizes third-party private certifiers. To learn more about organic livestock production, see the online *Organic Livestock Workbook* produced by NCAT. (***Resources**, p. 88.*)

USDA Legal Definitions
- ***Natural beef:*** No artificial additives, minimally processed.
- ***Organic beef:*** No hormones, antibiotics, pesticides, and fed only organically raised feed. For beef to be certified organic, the processor who renders it needs to be certified as well.

What makes this issue confusing is that customers have differing perceptions on what these terms mean. For instance, natural beef is considered by most people to be beef with no antibiotics and no steroids. Using the USDA definition, that isn't necessarily true.

Although most people can tell you what the term *free range* means, there is a great deal of confusion among consumers between *organic* and *natural*. You should be aware of how educated your customers are before going through all the trouble and cost of being organic.

Personally, I feel this will be the final chapter for the vague natural label. I predict that the term *natural* will start to fade away, as beef companies develop their specific certification programs.

Scheduling

Unlike marketing your cattle conventionally and selling everything on one day, direct marketing your beef will cause you to have to deliver cattle several times a year (***Entrepreneurs***, p. 44).

It can be trickier than you might think. If you are doing farmers markets, it is not so critical if you don't have beef to sell at every market (other than lost opportunity). However, if you are selling to stores and restaurants, you cannot ever run short. They will be willing to work with you from time to time, but if it becomes a habit, they'll stop buying from you. In fact, that will probably

be your biggest stumbling block to selling to restaurants and stores — earning their trust that you won't ever come up short.

If you've done your planning homework, you should be able to predict your demand close enough not to cause any major problems. Stores and restaurants have a very good idea of how your product will do with their customers. Be sure to flat out ask them what your sales volume might be, listen and respect their advice. We also make it a rule to have a major new client one full year before adding additional clients, so that we get a good feel for their demand cycles.

Choosing how to schedule your cattle production is important from a marketing perspective. Most urban customers are conditioned for convenience — they are used to buying tomatoes 365 days per year, rather than late summer when the tomatoes are ripe on the vine in our part of the world. This same thinking applies to cattle as well. Most urban customers do not realize that it takes two years to grow out beef, or that cattle only finish well during a certain part of the year.

It will be your job to either educate your customers about time and seasonal restraints, or develop a "pipeline" that will satisfy their need for the convenience of having grass-fed beef available 24/7.

There are basically only three ways to sell beef: 1) feedlot, 2) seasonally, and 3) frozen. Of course there could even be variations or

Natural beef is considered by most people to be beef with no antibiotics and no steroids. Using the USDA definition, that isn't necessarily true.

combinations of these three ways, but how you schedule your cattle will depend a lot on which way you choose.

The most forgiving of these three is frozen. Your frozen storage is your pipeline. You can theoretically finish all your beef in three months, throw it all in a freezer, and then sell it all year long. Of course there is some cost with this, and that needs to be figured into the equation. It also allows you to keep a cushion that will smooth out the bumps between supply and demand, or when bringing on a new customer.

We've never run a feedlot, but it seems to be the second easiest way. A lot is also a pipeline. The hard part is buying the right weights at the right time of year to feed your demand. To do this, you will either have to develop multiple breeding seasons, or buy from a large geographical area where folks don't all calve at the same time. You also don't have to plan so far in advance with a feedlot. Because more of your cattle will finish within a year, you can move and make changes faster. In a grass-fed program, it takes two years to finish an animal.

Finally, a seasonal product is hardest, at least from a scheduling point of view. It also has a lot of advantages in that your cattle are out on the pasture earning you money, instead of taking money eating bought feed or paying rent for frozen storage. However, you will have to stair-step your cattle to finish throughout the season. It's a pretty hard task in itself, not even considering all the other

Most urban customers do not realize that it takes two years to grow out beef, or that cattle only finish well during a certain part of the year.

elements that can frustrate you: differing rates of gain, sickness, drought, demand surges, predator kills, carcass variability and mechanical breakdowns at the slaughter house (even though the processing has stopped, your cattle are still going). With a seasonal program, once you get behind, things snowball fast and it's almost impossible to catch up.

To help us plan for the un-plannable, we forward contract our cattle as much as two years in advance. You can do this with direct marketing because you are in control of the carcass price and therefore also control the live price. See *Factors that Affect Your Bottom Line* (p. 84).

Learn How to Cook Your Beef

Since starting this business, we've found that we are an endangered species – people who cook and eat their own food! At first we took it for granted that people would know how to cook a variety of dishes, and would know the appropriate cut of beef for that dish. It's not true.

I can't tell you the number of times that we've had a customer call and complain about the toughness of their steak. After a little questioning, it usually turns out that they took a round steak, plunked it under the broiler and turned it into a hockey puck. Then they think our meat is tough. They usually try to tell us that they always cook round steak this way.

I think what really happens is that they go to the market, buy a slab of something red and do the easiest possible thing — broil the crud out of it. We bet that they never have any idea what cut they bought.

We have found that this is even more true for grass-fed beef. You don't have to apologize for anything, just tell them what to cook with what. Tell people specifically what cuts are good for what kinds of dishes. We even give away a little booklet, the *Holder Family's Favorite Recipes.* I thought that the recipes in there are just regular stuff, but people rave about them.

Cooking really comes in handy at farmers markets. Keep in mind that you will have to check the local, county and state regulations to see what they will allow. In one county where I sell and pass out samples at farmers markets, I don't need any kind of permit at all. In another county, I need a $15 permit. In yet another, it isn't allowed unless I am preparing the samples in a county-certified mobile kitchen. Make sure you check it out.

Anything you have a hard time moving can be sold at farmers markets — just cook samples and hand out recipe cards for the dish. When we do sampling in supermarkets (again, check regulations), we ask that the manager have pre-made ingredient kits available — people are thrilled to be able to just pick up a packet and go. Similarly, request that store managers stock extra of any ingredient found in your recipe. One day, we made fajitas for sampling. Even though we had asked the store manager

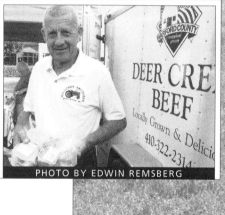

PHOTO BY EDWIN REMSBERG

to stock extra tortillas, peppers, etc., they sold out within an hour. The store not only lost a lot of sales but also had to contend with dozens of irritated customers.

Processing

Finding a processing facility can be really hard or really easy, depending where you live and what your needs are. Processing plants vary enormously in the types of processing they do. You need to have a pretty good idea of what your needs are before you go looking for a plant because the evaluation and site visits you'll need to do are very time-consuming.

Check your state Department of Agriculture for a list of facilities in your state. This list will tell you if the plant is state or federally inspected and whether it is a kill plant, a processing plant, or both. A kill plant actually kills the animals, hangs and chills them. A processing plant cuts up the carcasses.

First, target only the ones that do both killing and processing. You don't want to truck your meat from one plant to another if you can avoid it. Then call them up and find out exactly what they do. A lot of plants are very specialized and only serve a particular market.

Then go visit them. No matter what they tell you on the phone, nothing replaces a site inspection. Pay attention to the details. Are their offices clean? Are the employees happy? Strike up conversations with everyone you can. Ask them how long they have worked there, what they do, and how they like their jobs. Write down the names of their equipment; ask them about the throughput per hour, day and week in every area of the operation. Ask them who their customers are. Ask for references. Ask to meet their inspector.

The good plants will be very open. They will show you everything; they will be proud of their plant. The bad ones will be obvious after just the first few minutes. They won't want you talking to anyone. They will ask you why you need that information. They won't give you specifics. They will act insulted that you questioned their integrity.

Run away as fast as you can.

Once you have it narrowed down, get pricing on the work you want them to do. Be very specific. Tell them what products you want, exactly how you want them cut, how each cut is to be packaged, boxed and labeled, and where and when your shipment will be delivered.

For us, it was pretty hard. We needed a federally inspected plant (because our products cross state lines, and our client's insurance demanded federal, not state inspection), that could kill and custom-process. It also had to be able to separate our beef from other beef, because of our grass-fed label. We found only three federally inspected killing and processing facilities in the state that would custom-process for us. So keep in mind that even if your product doesn't cross state lines, you may still need a federally inspected plant.

We have found that with increasing frequency, a restaurant or store's insurance carrier requires them to only sell federally inspected products.

So don't assume that state inspection is acceptable unless you ask your potential client.

Most large federal plants will not deal with you. They aren't interested in cleaning their machines so that their meat does not contaminate yours. They do not want the hassle of having to keep your meat in a separate area from the conventional beef. They do not want your few animals gumming up their massive assembly line.

We now have most of our processing done at the University of Arizona Meat Science Lab. The plant is sparkling clean, it has great equipment, and the person who runs it has been very helpful to us.

Our jerky and marinated roasts are processed at another plant. We have to truck the meat in refrigerated vehicles. We are using a sausage and hot dog plant in Phoenix that does a great job and has a wonderful little old man offering you great samples.

However, the plants we use are okay for now, but not perfect. We cannot serve many clients because we do not have the right kind of processing available to us.

MAKING SURE YOU GET IT DONE RIGHT

Keeping an inventory of processed beef is next to impossible. The yield of every carcass is a little different, and you might cut up different carcasses differently. However, keeping good records keeps meat from disappearing.

We've created a form that helps us:
- Communicate with the processing plant about how we want our carcass cut.
- Create a visual check list to make sure we've accounted for the whole carcass.
- Inventory cut beef.
- Keep the processing plant honest.
- See trends to predict yields of certain cuts.
- Access written records if there is a problem.
- Create carcass performance data that can be taken to a breeder.

You may want to consider having your carcasses graded, at least occasionally, to help you learn more about your cattle. Our processor will do it for free on an unofficial basis. An official USDA grader charges a fee.

FEDERAL INSPECTORS

All federally inspected processing facilities will have a federal inspector who maintains a permanent office within the facility. They are always present when the slaughter is done and they regulate the way the meat is handled within the facility. They also enforce the rules concerning the transfer of meat between

facilities. For instance, if you transfer meat from a federally inspected facility to a state-inspected facility, it is then considered only state-inspected.

Like everyone else, there are good inspectors and bad inspectors. Yet, every one of them wields a lot of power. Most of their interaction will be with the operators of the processing plant, but you will need to deal with them a little. Be nice to them. They can be a great help, or they can make your life miserable. For instance, the amount of meat that you can give away is actually regulated. Samples are all supposed to be marked "sample," and the amount may not exceed 2,000 pounds per year. Now, if you have a good relationship with your inspector, he probably is not going to inspect and count each and every sample that you take from the processing plant, but he certainly has the power to do so.

Getting a Label

If you plan on having your product cross state lines, you have to have a federal label. A federal label can only come from a federally inspected plant. Your label is attached to your processing plant. For instance, we have a separate label for our jerky and marinated roasts than for our other beef products. They look almost the same. The only difference is the establishment number in the circle in the lower-right corner. That's it. The plant that does your processing will apply to the

> Like everyone else, there are good inspectors and bad inspectors. Yet, every one of them wields a lot of power ... so be nice to them.

federal government for your label. You need to have the artwork created – preferably on a computer, so that changes can be made easily – then give it to your processing house to have it approved. Some plants will provide this service for you, usually at no charge.

Obtaining approval on your label can take as little as 10 days, or many months, depending on how out of the ordinary your label is and the experience of the processing company.

When we applied for our first federal label, it took quite a while. Our processing house had never applied for a label with anything strange like natural on it. Even adding that fairly innocuous word apparently makes the feds nervous. Our label kept being rejected over and over, and we couldn't figure out why.

Finally, out of desperation, we hired a label expediter to help get our label through. An expediter is a person who knows all the guys in Washington who fret over the terms like natural and organic and hormone-free. He gets paid a lot of money for knowing where their offices are and what questions to ask when they tell him that your label was rejected. And, most amazing, he can tell you exactly what to change so that the label will pass. After months and months of going around and around with our label, it turned out that what was wrong was frustratingly simple. We stated on the label – "Keep Refrigerated or Frozen." It turns out that we can say, "Keep Refrigerated" or "Keep Frozen," but not both. How could we have

> If you plan on having your product cross state lines, you have to have a federal label. A federal label can only come from a federally inspected plant. Your label is attached to your processing plant.

been so misinformed? Actually, in the end it was not really very expensive (a couple hundred dollars), and we should have hired the expediter a lot sooner.

While I would never claim to entirely understand the label approval office, they seem to be getting more user-friendly. You can find out more about labels and getting your approval at www.fsis.usda.gov/home. If you want to sell your product as certified organic, your label as well as your processing plant also will have to be approved by your state or third party certifier.

The easy thing to do is to team up with a processing house with experience dealing with natural or organic labels or copy one that has already been approved. Don't try to do your advertising with your product label. You will never win in a battle with federal regulators. Make all your claims on your point-of-purchase material or your product literature, not on your federal label. Anything that you say on your federal label has to be approved by the feds. That is time-consuming, at best.

If you want to say that your beef is better for you, say it in your brochures. If you want to say that your beef is tender, say it in your brochures. If you put it in your brochures, it's just your business. If it's on your federal label, it's the feds' business.

Obtaining approval on your label can take as little as 10 days, or many months, depending on how out of the ordinary your label is and the experience of the processing company.

LABEL SOURCES

When you're first starting out, especially when you are still deciding what your product mix will be, go to a small printing company for your labels. You want to order pressure-sensitive labels that come on continuous-feed rolls. Your quantities will be too small for a regular label company to be cost-effective. Most small printing companies sub-contract with a to-the-trade-only label printer.

Make all your labels the same color (although you can create screens of one color for more visual interest) and try to do them all at once. You may have different quantities of each – 1,000 stew beef labels, 500 sirloin steak labels, 500 tenderloin steak labels, and 3,000 ground beef labels. Go with a standard size, as custom sizes are a lot more expensive. Sizes usually run in 1-inch increments.

When your volume is higher (such as 10,000 labels or more), deal directly with a label printing company. Most major metropolitan areas have one or two. Look in the yellow pages. Get bids from two or three if possible. Make sure to give them the following information: quantity of each label, total quantity, size, ink color, color of stock (the paper that the labels are printed on), whether the labels need to be waterproof, and delivery location. Expect a four-week turnaround time.

Packaging Your Product

Bulk ground beef is most economically packaged in small bags, usually referred to as chubb bags. They come in 1-, 2- and 5-pound sizes, and you can select from different thicknesses of plastic. You can buy them pre-printed with some standard design, and then have your label affixed when they are filled at the processing plant. When your quantities are higher (5,000 and above), you can have your label pre-printed on the bag. There are only a few chubb bag companies around. Don't purchase really cheap bags, as cheap bags tend to get holes during the filling process. Seek food service equipment and supplies sources online.

Recently, we have changed our ground beef packaging to a Styrofoam tray with a perishable food wrapping. Our processor still occasionally had trouble with pin holes in the chubb bags. Even though it is more expensive, in the end it made our customers and us happier, not to have packages that had to be returned due to defects.

Most consumers will not buy a product that they cannot see, especially if they've never bought it before. So package your beef in clear plastic perishable food wrapping, vacuum packed. It is more expensive, but important not only so the consumer can see what he or she is getting, but also so the product stays fresh longer. Food wrapping, such as Cryovac®, gives meat a longer shelf life than paper-wrapped meat. The higher cost is offset by these benefits.

Package your beef in convenient sizes. We have found that the person who typically buys our product tends to eat smaller portions than your average meat consumer. At the supermarket, ground beef is usually sold in 1 ½- to 2-pound packages. Our customers complained that that was too large. So now we sell our ground beef, ground beef patties, stew beef, and fajita beef in 1-pound packages, steaks two-to-a-package, tenderloin at ¾ of a pound per package, New York strips at 1 pound per package, rib eyes at 1 pound, 3 ounces per package, roasts at 3 pounds each and beef jerky at 1 ounce per package.

If you wind up selling to a distribution source — such as a restaurant, natural foods distribution company, or a retail store — instead of directly to a consumer, they will inquire about case sizes. Generally we have found it is best to have a case big enough that the cost of cardboard doesn't kill you, but it won't mean too large of an investment in one order.

PHOTO BY BOB CUNNINGHAM

Also, weight is a factor. A lot of women are employed as warehouse workers these days. Don't make up cases weighing over 35 or 40 pounds. Our cases are usually 24 pounds. You need to label all cases with the product codes (we use the standard codes listed in the beef buyers guide unless we have come up with a cut that is not listed — then we make up our own).

UPC CODES

Some retailers want you to include bar coding or a Universal Product Code (UPC). That is the little code on your product that identifies your company and its location to the store, and may contain other information including the product price. Bar coding is new for meat products. We have never had a client insist upon it, which is good, as it does add cost to the bottom line.

There are many websites that detail how to get a bar code onto your label. Any processed product (such as hot dogs, jerky, etc.) will require a UPC code. Some producers join the Universal Product Code organization, which charges a one-time fee. The Universal Product Code association is on the Internet at www.uc-council.org.

A ranching friend buys all his bar codes from a private company he finds cheaper and faster: www.buyabarcode.com. Their one-time fee of $75 is a bargain compared to the $800 charged by the UPC Council, and the bar codes are only $35 each. Moreover, you don't have to sort through new software to download a code.

Then, consider three ways to get your bar code on your product:

- Contact a printing company that prints UPC bar code labels, which can then be applied to your product.
- Have a UPC bar code printed directly on the package of your product.
- Print UPC bar code labels yourself using off-the-shelf software.

INSURANCE

Some of your customers — mostly retail stores, restaurants and some farmers markets — will require you to carry product liability insurance. This is a separate policy from your normal ranch or farm insurance. It's not all that big of a deal. Most places require $1 million in liability. Present a "certificate of insurance" to your client whenever you meet them for the first time. If they demand it, it will save some time. If they don't, you will look all the more respectable and trustworthy.

Genetics

There are a ton of different breeds of cattle out there. If you read the breeds marketing literature, they all seem to "calve well, gain fast, and do great under range conditions." Of course, if this were true, we'd only need one breed of cow. In reality, we all live in different climates, and we are all looking for certain strengths in our cattle — even more so for you as a niche marketer.

For example, meat marbling is definitely one of those personal preference issues. Some particularly health-conscious customers don't want any marbling in their beef. Others claim their beef isn't tender without a little fat. You'll need to discern what most of your customers like and plan your breeds accordingly.

One more thing you also will hear is, "There are more differences within a breed than between breeds." There is an element of truth to this. By the same token, you will never find a Zebu that marbles as well as a Wygu. The moral here again is only you will know what's best for you. Based on what we learned about genetics and our experiences, we've made some basic conclusions.

Cattle that marble well:
- Angus
- Jersey
- Hereford
- Red Angus
- Highlanders
- Murry Grey
- Tarantaise

I've read that Highlands cattle marble very easily; they have so much hair, they don't need any back fat and put that energy in marbling.

Leaner cattle with less marbling:
- Zebu
- Brahma
- Brangus
- Gelbvieh
- Braunvieh

I have heard that there is a strain of Brahma that is very tender. Personally, I have had very bad luck with them, as tenderness goes. Only about 4 percent have been tender enough.

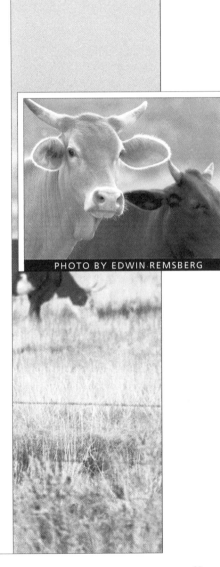
PHOTO BY EDWIN REMSBERG

The longer we are in this business, the more respect we have for genetics. Good genetics has a lot to do with the tenderness of your beef. Angus cattle can make just as many tough steaks as a Brahma. It just depends on the genetics behind them. Good genetics also has a lot to do with profitability. There is a 20-percent difference between our best cattle and our worst in the weight of our high-end cuts.

Another area we are working with is maturity. Maturity is based on frame size, but knowing when an animal has matured (and, more importantly, marbled) is as much of an art as a science. It's just a skill you have to develop. However, there are some basics.

No matter how much you feed your animals or how good the forage is, they will not start to marble until they mature. Currently, the conventional market is looking for animals maturing at 1,200 to 1,300 pounds. This seems ludicrous. The only person to profit on such heavy weights is the feeder (who gets to sell more feed), and the packer (who gets a break by spreading his hard costs over a heavier animal).

For a grass-fed product, we are looking at something that will mature in two years or less. After about 30 months of age, you will start running into tenderness problems related solely to age (this isn't a hard and fast rule, with good genetics we've been able to slaughter open three-year-olds with no tenderness problems). With that in mind, we've been looking to raise an animal that will mature at 800 to 1,000 pounds, a figure sort of pulled out of a hat. Maybe 600 to 800 pounds is the magic figure. We chose 800 to 1,000 pounds because it seemed do-able without getting into an extreme breeding program.

> For a grass-fed product, we are looking at something that will mature in two years or less.

As our genetics and quality of forage improves, we are experimenting with trying to take this weight up to 1,000 to 1,100 pounds. The jury is still out on whether this is economical. If you buy calves instead of producing your own, you may want to choose the shorter frame animals that will mature at your lighter harvest weight.

Ultimately, we believe these new breeding programs will be a spin-off industry of grass-fed beef. Beef that do well in a feedlot don't necessarily do well on grass. Special breeding lines will have to be created. Grass-fed cattle in Minnesota will be very different genetically from Florida, or Arizona, or anywhere else. We all have different situations and needs. We will all need different genetics, and someone, somewhere will supply them.

Forage

All forage is not created equal. You can work to improve both the amount and quality of your feed. Each season, we work to improve our pasture, and a large part of that is managing how the forage is harvested.

> All forage is not created equal. You can work to improve both the amount and quality of your feed. Each season, we work to improve our pasture, and a large part of that is managing how the forage is harvested.

You'll want to put your brood cows on your poorest forage. Granted, they will do better on better forage, but to get the biggest bang for your buck, you'll want to save your good forage for your high-value animals, those you are finishing. These animals are gaining in weight and quality, as opposed to your cow herd, which is depreciating and doesn't get as much of a benefit out of good forage. Some intensive graziers even do a leader/follower system.

In beginning our grass-fed program, we didn't worry too much about forages. We used all native forage that was already in the fields. In fact, some producers report raising great-tasting beef from native grasses, which also saves them money. However, our experience is leading us to believe there may be enough value in planted forages to warrant more research.

We are looking at finishing our animals with high-energy forage. Here is a list, ranked highest to lowest:

- brassicas
- legumes
- cool-season annuals
- perennial ryegrass
- warm-season annuals
- cool-season perennials
- alfalfa

Most of the grass-fed world (Argentina, New Zealand) concentrates on the top four. In taste tests in Alabama, California and England, ryegrass was found to produce a better tasting beef than grain. However, while fescue was almost universally disliked, it can be a useful piece of your system.

No one knows the minimum amount of time an animal has to be finished on high quality forage. There have been some figures thrown about ranging anywhere from

50 to 100 days, but no one really knows. Again, native grasses might prove an attractive, low-cost option.

One thing we do know comes from Dr. Dick Diven, of the Low Cost Cow/Calf Production School: When your steer reaches 60 percent of its mature body weight, it will be at a point in its development where it grows intramuscular fat (marbling) cells or connective tissue (gristle). If your steer is on an upward plane of nutrition (gaining weight), it will form marbling cells. If not, it will form connective tissue. This is one reason you can't look at a fat steer ready for slaughter and predict if he'll marble well. Unless you know how he was doing when he hit 60 percent of his mature weight, you can feed him all you want and he still won't marble.

Dr. Diven also has a word of caution if you are using grain to supplement your grass program. Without going into the complex rumen chemistry, oil grains (like cotton seed or soy) will work more efficiently with the rumen, allowing the steer to eat more cheap grass. A starch grain (like corn) will work against the rumen in a grass-based program, making the rumen, in time, more dependent on bought grain for its nutritional needs.

People who market sustainably raised food in innovative ways provide inspirational real-life models. Consider adapting ideas from the approaches that follow.

entrepreneurs

With more than a century of sheep ranching tradition on their 30,000-acre central Oregon ranch, Dan and Jeanne Carver wanted to continue raising sheep despite declining lamb and wool markets. With a grant from the Sustainable Agriculture Research and Education (SARE) program, they researched markets and launched a product line featuring uniqueness and quality.

Today, their sales include lamb for high-end restaurants, wool in yarn-and-pattern kits for hand knitters, and ready-to-wear woolen and lambskin fashions. These sideline enterprises augment the main ranch commodities, which include 800 head of cattle, hay, and 3,000 acres of no-till grain.

With a lack of processors, the Carvers were forced to find custom outfits willing to develop out-of-the-ordinary retail products. They found a small meat processor 80 miles away and attracted restaurants using many messages — fresh, locally grown, "natural" spring lamb from a ranch awarded for its conservation practices. "That's a lot of sizzle," said Jeanne.

Once washed and dyed, the wool becomes yarn for kits featuring the Carvers' knitwear designs and is sold through a dealer who publishes a catalog circulated to 100,000 crafters. Repeated requests for finished garments from their wool encouraged Jeanne to work with area designers and knitters to create handmade woolen clothing sold in resorts and specialty shops. To use the whole animal, they began tanning hides and added lambskin fashion items to their clothing line.

"The marketing project has increased awareness and visibility of what we grow, how we grow it and, most importantly, how we manage the land," said Dan, referring to a bevy of practices to safeguard the environment, such as installing miles of fencing to control grazing impact and building dams to create watering holes for domestic stock and wildlife.

Lamb sales have spurred interest in their beef, which the Carvers primarily sell as 700-pound calves to the generic market. With the new interest from lamb buyers, however, they now direct-market their finished beef to some of their established lamb customers and high-end restaurants dotting the Columbia River Gorge.

Dan said they only direct-market about 50 head of beef a year, but not for lack of interest. "Once the chefs tour the ranch and see the roots of their product, they ask 'How do we get your beef?'" he said. "The demand is there for increased direct-market sales but it will grow only as fast as our processing and distribution will allow."

The Carvers estimate they clear 30 percent over the price

of lamb sold on the generic market, and wool profits are growing even while they keep prices affordable.

"Our customers love the quality of our product, the flavor profile of the meat, the feel of the wool and the message of the land and sense of place," Jeanne said.

THE CARVER FAMILY
2002 SARE PROGRAM GRANT RECIPIENT

Written by Valerie Berton | Image from Dan and Jean Carver

Bill and Di Hodge had raised a small cattle herd in addition to their "day jobs" for decades, but got serious about making the sideline activity a real income-generating enterprise after they saw the potential of marketing grass-fed beef.

"Six to eight years ago, we suddenly came to the realization that a cow was put on this Earth to graze," said Bill Hodge, an extension educa-

tor who farms in northwest Georgia. "We wanted to see if we could produce a consumer-acceptable product from pasture."

After four years of forage research, the Hodges had perfected a system of growing cold-season and warm-season grasses that not only performed well in their climate but also produced a good flavor in their beef. They introduced customers to their new product at a nearby farmers market in Carrollton started in 2002 partly with support from a Sustainable Agriculture Research and Education (SARE) program grant.

The Cotton Mill Farmers Market filled a gap in northwest Georgia. As a suburban population drifted west from Atlanta during the 1990s, Carroll County grew. Many of the new residents knew nothing about the local farm products. SARE's grant supported a new market initiated by civic groups, government agencies and farmers committed to bridging that gap.

As Carroll County extension director, Hodge participated in the local effort to launch the market. In 2003, its second year, the market featured 32 producers, the Hodges among them. The market was an ideal venue to test their packaging scheme devised to use the whole animal: 20-, 30- and 40-pound packs of ground beef, steaks and roasts.

That season the farmers market became a primary sales outlet for the Hodges, especially with the opportunity to feature their beef in occasional chef demonstrations prepared on site.

"The farmers market gave us a venue to be in the market and expose the product," Bill said. "It really made a difference [to customers] to have a chef prepare our beef, with the aroma flowing through the market."

Today, the Hodges sell their meat under their "Hodge Common Sense Beef" label directly from their farm or on online at websites like LocalHarvest.org and EatWild.com, where Hodge says they have gained many customers. They still go to the Cotton Mill market sometimes, but say demand now exceeds supply from their herd of 40.

The Hodges have begun marketing meat for several producers under their label. "Others don't want to spend the time dealing with the public," Bill said. "There's a lot of time and energy involved in direct marketing."

Despite that, the Hodges still sell at the market periodically. They expect to diversify and offer lamb from a new flock of sheep and are considering goats as a biological weed control on their land.

THE HODGE FAMILY
BENEFITED FROM A 2002 SARE PROGRAM GRANT

Written by Valerie Berton | Image from Wendy Crager

For eight years, Bill and Denise Brownlee watched feed prices rise and pork prices fall, wondering all the while how they could make their Wil-Den Family Farms in Pennsylvania more profitable. In 2002, they decided to exploit what they saw as a market advantage — for years they have perfected an outdoor production system where their hogs farrow and finish on pasture without growth stimulants and minimal antibiotic use. The Brownlees withdrew their pork from conventional sales and began trying to market their product directly to customers.

Given the time commitment involved in direct marketing, they scaled back their operation from 170 sows to 60 and began focusing on selling 900 to 1,000 animals per year, this time at a premium. Their broad efforts include developing a meat-oriented community agriculture project, running a subscription service, partnering with CSA farmers, selling at farmers markets and grocery stores, selling to institutions, and establishing an on-farm store.

With help from a grant from the Sustainable Agriculture Research and Education (SARE) program to a local non-profit organization that wanted to test the concept of a community-supported agriculture project focused on meat, the Brownlees began hosting meat sampling events. They hoped to capture 100 families interested in buying annual "shares" of their farm product. For between $400 and $800, depending on their choices, each member would receive a mix: bone-in center-cut chops, bacon, ground pork, breakfast sausage, Italian sausage and semi-boneless ham, throughout the year. The concept, however, failed to take hold.

"We tried to pattern it after how people are used to buying from vegetable farmers: paying up-front," Denise said. "For whatever reason, they were hesitant to commit." They changed their strategy to encourage people to buy a month's supply of meat in a subscription service and hope their happy customers will begin buying for a full year. About 40 customers have subscribed for monthly meat deliveries.

Denise and Bill host meat sampling at a variety of venues. Denise's first presentation at a local business gained a handful of customers, who are still receiving meat deliveries.

A local restaurant featured the Brownlees, a beef producer and a poultry farmer in a pastured meat tasting. And at a nearby conservatory, they took part in a "Green Eats" event, distributing tastes of pork to a well-heeled crowd.

Early successes include selling whole hogs, an inexpensive way to move the entire animal, to institutions such as a convent and ground pork to Washington and Jefferson College in

Washington, Pa. Selling lower-end cuts remains one of their biggest challenges.

"We've doubled the pigs we slaughter under our label, but it's not enough," Denise said. "We have just 60 sows paying the bills and we need to make more money from those animals."

THE BROWNLEE FAMILY
BENEFITED FROM A 2004 SARE PROGRAM GRANT

Written by Valerie Berton | Image from Bill & Denise Brownlee

Since 1999, Wende Elliott has raised poultry and lamb in a pasture-based system on her 120-acre central Iowa farm. With her husband, Joe Rude, she gained organic certification for her meat products, as well as alfalfa, oats and corn.

As they fine-tuned their production, Wende and Joe pondered how to get the most from their meat. In 2001, Wende wrote a business plan and successfully

launched a cooperative called Wholesome Harvest. With two grants from the Sustainable Agriculture Research and Education (SARE) program, she began to promote meat sales in five Midwestern states.

Wholesome Harvest is now a thriving, farmer-owned organic business with more than 40 members. The e-commerce site, wholesomeharvest.com, is a successful direct sales mechanism that augments more traditional markets such as grocery stores and restaurants.

The website provides a wealth of information about the Wholesome Harvest cooperative and the group's efforts to promote organic meat grown on pasture with humane handling practices.

Wholesome Harvest's virtual market enables buyers to order meat online for delivery. It evolved from Wende's vision that people who wanted to eat certified organic, independently raised meat from family farms didn't have to go farther than their computer to shop for it.

In an innovative twist on community agriculture projects, people can join Wholesome Harvest's meat-of-the-month club and receive monthly shipments of organic beef, chicken, lamb, duck, goose and turkey, much like a CSA. Frozen meat on dry ice is shipped via two-day express delivery.

In its advertising, the co-op emphasizes that its products are locally grown, farmer-owned, pasture-raised and rendered at custom processors to give them a human edge over the more anonymous industrial model.

"We can't compete on cheap food," Wende said, "but we can compete on quality and freshness and the fact that our product is local."

Growth, the co-op's communications officer says, is steady. For that and other reasons, Wende hopes to form a national coalition of regional organic meat cooperatives.

"Only by working together can farmers protect the added value of organic meat, and capture premium and remote as well as mainstream markets for their products," Wende said. "Otherwise, they will end up being paid what the plant wants to pay them."

To learn more about the national coalition, contact Wende at welliott@wholesomeharvest.com.

THE ELLIOTT/RUDE FAMILY
2000 & 2002 SARE PROGRAM GRANT RECIPIENT

Written by Valerie Berton | Image from Wholesome Harvest

THE HATFIELD FAMILY
OREGON NATURAL BEEF

There were two pioneers in the direct marketing beef business: Mel Coleman of Coleman Beef, and Doc and Connie Hatfield of Oregon Natural Beef. Mel basically modeled his production system after the conventional market and had mixed results (for a more detailed analysis, read his book *Riding the Higher Range*). The Hatfields, however, truly blazed their own trail.

In a nutshell, they created a cooperative of producers who promise a certain number of cattle during different parts of the year. These cattle are then fed out and slaughtered, with the owner retaining ownership. At slaughter, the slaughter house buys the beef for conventional prices, but stores the beef separately from their conventional beef. The Hatfields then get on the phone to their clients and take orders for that week. With orders in hand, they then buy back as much of their beef as demand will allow from the processing facility. Then they pay the producer a premium for the amount of beef they were able to sell.

The nice part of this model is that there is a steady supply of fresh beef and a guaranteed sale. At the very least, you'd get what you would have gotten by selling your cattle conventionally. Finally, it makes producers more conscious of the product they offer.

STRENGTH: *Year-round production, guaranteed sale*

WEAKNESS: *High production/start-up cost*

THE JAMES FAMILY
JAMES RANCH GRASS-FINISHED BEEF

The James family, like the Salatins, has made a nice living doing things on a smaller scale. They slaughter their beef at around 950-1,150 pounds, the majority in the late fall, but also some in the spring. The beef is then frozen and sold throughout the year. Part of their marketing is done through an on-ranch store that is open one day a week. Another part is sold at a local farmers market. They also sell most of their hamburger through some high-end local restaurants who cater to tourists looking for a western experience as well as natural food groceries in and near Durango.

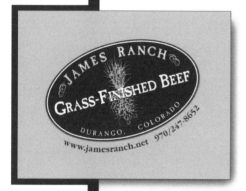

James Ranch beef cattle begin their lives on pastures in Utah and are then moved to the ranch to graze on cool-season grasses and clovers. The Red Angus beef cattle grow quickly on grass and are ready for market between 18 and 30 months of age.

Besides grass-finished beef, the multi-generational family operation also produces artisan cheese and pastured pork.

The Jameses advertise their meat online at www.jamesranch.net. There, customers can pre-order beef using an online order form and pick it up in Durango.

STRENGTH: *Low start-up and production cost*

WEAKNESS: *Time spent away from the ranch at store or in market*

THE HOLDER FAMILY
ERVIN'S GRASSFED BEEF

Will and I started Ervin's Grassfed Beef (EGB) in 1997. The company was named after my husband Will's maternal grandfather, Ervin Hicks (*below*), who had a wonderful land ethic and a gentle way with animals. Originally, we tried to form a cooperative, including our neighbors and a few other ranchers who do a great job with their land and their cattle. Unfortunately, even though everyone agreed that it was a great idea, no one but us was willing to spend any money or time developing it. So now, our program is set up like a cooperative, at least in spirit. On paper, EGB is simply a marketing agent that buys cattle from other ranchers who are willing to adhere to the same set of standards that we do. This way, EGB is a pretty lean organization, giving most of the value to the producer and the consumer.

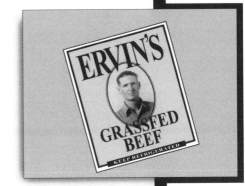

Each rancher with whom we work is certified by EGB to meet the standards we advertise to the consumer. They are responsible for the product and retain ownership until the steer is on the rail. Some producers don't want the responsibility of finishing a steer, so our ranch buys them from the producer (similar to a stocker operation), and sells them to EGB.

EGB offers three prices: hamburger (cull cow), stew beef (tough steer) and steak (tender steer). We only buy what our demand calls for. Originally, we started offering only a frozen product but have since been able to offer fresh as well.

STRENGTH: *Starting with frozen product is very forgiving and maximizes per carcass net*

WEAKNESS: *Frozen product limits marketability*

selling product

Situational Analysis

The first thing that you have to do is to identify your strengths and weaknesses. This sounds really simple, but we've found that it actually takes quite a bit of time. We wasted a lot of time trying to follow the models of some pretty brilliant people, only to get a ways down the road and find out that, given our particular set of circumstances, we couldn't go that route. So first off, do your homework. Make a list of what you have to work with.

Your team:
- Your family's background. This is a group effort.
- Your personality. How do you deal with others? Would you enjoy making a "cold" sales call?
- Your education and experience.

Your physical resources:
- The size of your ranch.
- The number and breed of cattle.
- The ranch's history, layout, elevation and character.
- If pesticides, non-organic fertilizers or herbicides have been used.
- If any part is irrigated or able to be irrigated.
- The condition of the pastures.
- Water availability.
- If you own, or have access to, scales.

Your location:
- The distance to a town.
- The distance to a major metropolitan area.
- The nearest processing facility – and its willingness to train you.

Economics:
- Your economic situation. Do you have savings to support you during transition?
- How much money does the ranch need to produce, both short and long term?
- How much cash reserve do you have?
- What is your available credit?
- Can you afford to break even or even lose money for a few years? The general rule is to expect seven years to establish a profitable direct-market business.

Supporting resources such as:
- Small Business Development Centers. The U.S. Small Business Administration runs these programs to provide management assistance to current and prospective small business owners. www.sba.gov/sbdc/
- Extension staff with experience in direct meat marketing.
- Private consultants.

Answer all of these questions before you proceed. Every factor will play a part in deciding what type of operation is the best for you. For example, if you are located fairly close to a metropolitan area, your family has some experience with direct sales, and you like dealing with people, the Joel Salatin model may be the best for you. Then again, if you don't like direct sales, and you are located way out in the boonies, then you may want to have a distributor sell for you.

You may want to consider writing a business plan. For help, consult *Building a Sustainable Business*, a handbook from the Sustainable Agriculture Network (**Resources**, p. 89).

Sales Outlets
RESTAURANTS

Restaurants use a lot of beef. It seems, then, that they would be an excellent avenue to market your product. They must have small margins, though, because they are the most price-conscious customers that we have. They also want it in particular ways. It seems that every type of restaurant has its own particular needs.

You are probably wasting your time working with franchise restaurants. Locally owned restaurants are more likely to share your goals.

Mexican restaurants use a lot of beef, but the problem is that they use a lot of very cheap beef — the stew, rounds, brisket, skirt, plate and ground beef. We have found that even the ones who advertise healthy food with low fat still buy 60-cent-a-pound ground beef. You have to look for the kinds of restaurants that offer a healthy, ecologically sensitive and high-ticket menu.

PHOTO BY EDWIN REMSBERG

Restaurateurs also usually want fresh, not frozen, beef. That means frequent deliveries and a convenient delivery system. They also want a uniform product. The last thing a restaurant manager wants is a customer complaining that last time he ordered this steak it was a lot bigger (or leaner, or more tender, or whatever). However, things are changing. We have found that some restaurants will accept some product variability. They are the restaurants that already buy organic vegetables and seasonal, locally produced wines and breads. The best thing is that they are usually rather expensive, too. They are used to paying extra for what they want.

Search for chefs who will work closely with you. These kinds of chefs can creatively use many different cuts and will probably teach you a lot.

Some restaurants (generally those that specialize in organic and local fare) are willing to work with a number of small producers, but they are few and far between. They generally change their menus daily or weekly. When they get a specialty item like your tenderloin, they may want to feature it that evening while it lasts. So you need to give them notice when you will have high-end cuts so they can plan with the rest of their small suppliers.

Don't forget that high-end restaurants like lots of bones to make stock, generally more than just you can supply. It also is a nice idea to give them a few pounds of burger or roast occasionally that they can use for their staff dinners, which many host prior to serving hours. It always helps to make friends with the general staff.

STORES

You think the cattle business is tough? Spend an hour with a store buyer. They are thorough, knowledgeable, and so slick with a calculator you'll wonder where all your math education went to. These people are like commodity brokers. They deal in

> When restaurants get a specialty item like your tenderloin, they may want to feature it that evening while it lasts. So you need to give them notice when you will have high-end cuts.

tenths of percents. They are bottom line kind of people. If you are not completely buttoned up when you go to meet with these guys, they will not only chew you up, but feel angry that they wasted 15 minutes of their day on you.

Actually, they may not be that bad. However, don't go in thinking your sweet picture of a family farm is going to win them over. That picture is very important, but so are economics, margins and markups. Know all your costs going in – transportation, storage, delivery and pallet charges.

All of this might discourage you. Don't let it. Stores are wonderful in that, instead of having 200 customers, with 200 checks and 200 delivery times every month, you only have one. That decreases the headaches and day-to-day problems quite a bit.

Stores charge a mark up of about 30 percent – less in big supermarkets, more in small specialty stores. They will expect you to ask about their markup, and how and when they want your product delivered (and possibly by whose trucks).

Store buyers will ask you about:
- Customers
- Current gross sales
- When you can start delivery
- Case size
- What your product will look like (label, package, appearance)
- Promotional materials
- Liability insurance

PHOTO BY BOB CUNNINGHAM

DISTRIBUTORS

Distributors are a lot like stores, but with even bigger volume. For you, they are one customer, requiring one bill and one delivery, that does a ton of volume. The only bad thing is that your product is more costly to the consumer. Distributors charge anywhere from 8 to 30 percent, which jacks up your price considerably when you figure the retail store will add another 30 to 40 percent on top of that.

It seems that every major metropolitan area has a host of distributors that could be lumped into one of two categories:

1) big volume/little service, and 2) big service/lower volume. Big volume distributors are companies like Shamrock Foods who will want to deal with thousands of pounds of product at a time. For most family ranches (especially at start up), this is not a viable option.

> Distributors are a lot like stores, but with even bigger volume. For you, they are one customer, requiring one bill and one delivery, that does a ton of volume. The only bad thing is that your product is more costly to the consumer.

The big service distributors, which are harder to find, are willing to deal with much smaller quantities (even tens of pounds). These companies are either small Mom-and-Pop operations who have somehow managed to survive from the 1950s, or gourmet-type people. The easiest way to find them is to call the purchaser (they are also sometimes called "foragers" or "buying agents") of very exclusive restaurants and ask them who distributes their gourmet or hard-to-find items. Another nice reason for finding a gourmet distributor is that they are always looking for something new and novel to sell, such as your locally produced beef. Price isn't nearly as big an issue for them as it is with large-volume distributors. Again, you will have to weigh the good versus the bad and decide based upon your situation.

FARMERS MARKETS

If you live within easy driving distance of a city, farmers markets can be great. The investment is minimal, and you get paid immediately. It's really fun to boot. We always met a lot of nice customers and other vendors with natural products to sell. I would come home after a farmers market with the most wonderful breads, jams, produce and advice on what to do about our dog's arthritis.

The amount of money that you make is largely dependent upon the area you live in. The farmers markets in Phoenix aren't very well established yet. People don't seem to really use them for their regular shopping. We did meet quite a few nice people who became excellent regular customers. We believe that if we wanted to continue with the markets, we would have eventually built up a large amount of business. The amount of money we made in a day would have been fine if it was a half-hour drive for us, but it was more like six hours. Each way. That makes for an exhausting trip. Moreover, it was impossible for us to bring along our toddler son for that many hours, especially in Phoenix's brutal heat.

PHOTO BY EDWIN REMSBERG

SELLING PRODUCT

Tucson's markets are a lot better. There is one near an affluent area where a friend of ours sells out each week. It's only 45 minutes from her home. There are many other cities with huge, very successful farmers markets, so it's worth investigation.

The laws governing farmers markets vary depending upon where you live. In some areas, the county makes the rules. In some areas it is the state. In some areas you have to comply with the health department's rules and regulations. Some markets have tables and umbrellas for you to use, free of charge. Some don't. Some have access to power, some don't. Some let you sell out of traditional ice chests, some want electric-powered ice chests. They are all different.

We keep it fairly simple at our farmers markets: a folding table (we already had that), a cash box (we bought a plastic one for $6), and two electric ice chests (which we bought at a discount chain for $60 each), that we have used so much that we should have bought them years ago. If you can find them, glass-top ice cream display freezers work very well at farmers markets.

Begin by visiting the markets you are interested in trying. Ask market managers what rules and regulations you need to comply with. The reason for asking the markets and not the government agencies is that every agency always seems to think that they have the authority. I talked to 14 (no, I am not kidding) different people,

each of whom insisted that we had to follow a different set of rules. Some of them were downright ridiculous. One told me that we had to have a refrigerated truck and all people manning the booth had to be cleared by his department.

For the real low-down on the rules, ask the market manager or the vendors. They know what works and what doesn't.

Usually, the operators of the market receive a percentage of sales for providing the space setup and power. This percentage varies by market. I have heard that some charge a flat fee. In any case the charge is very small, usually between 3 to 5 percent.

In many areas you'll need a business license (so you'll have the privilege of paying taxes on your sales), and nothing else. We have been told that if we didn't raise the beef ourselves, it would mean that we are distributors, and insurance is more expensive. Most areas require $1 million in liability insurance. Check with your town, county and state authorities for regulations.

Selling products (or even giving away samples), that are cooked will also get you involved in a different set of rules and regulations (all of a sudden you're a restaurant), so stick to selling refrigerated or frozen beef unless the market manager gives his approval.

The opening and closing times vary a lot, too. Some are early markets, open from about six in the morning to about noon,

and some are geared to the business crowd, open for about three hours in the middle of the day. They expect you to be set up one-half hour before opening, and not leave until the official closing time. You need to make your own change, and have your own bags (here's a great use for all those plastic grocery sacks). Bring your brochures and print up a big (hand written) price list, and you are set to go. A few ideas to help sales:

- Display your product
- Display pricing
- Give out samples
- Hang a bright, easy-to-read sign
- Be outgoing

Consider publications like *The New Farmers' Market* and the *Growing for Market* newsletter (**Resources**, p. 88).

MAIL ORDER

We have tried mail order using frozen beef, and it's difficult in the Southwest, especially in the warm months. It requires very expensive special packaging, and either frozen gel packs or dry ice.

We have found that the packaging and shipping (because you have to ship overnight mail) usually far exceeds the value of the product. The small producer will not have the huge volumes that allow you to negotiate less expensive rates with the shipping companies. A large mail order company such as Walnut Creek can ship a package for $4 that would cost you or me $20.

If you want your product to retain its federal-inspection status, you have to package all shipments at a federally inspected plant. We have tried it, but we have not been able to make it work.

If you are going to offer a shelf-stable product, such as beef jerky, mail order can be a viable option. You can go in two different directions — sending out your own catalogs and filling orders directly, or advertising your beef in an already existing catalog and having them fulfill the orders for you.

DIRECT MAIL

If you want to try it yourself, you will need three things: an inexpensive, part-time labor pool, a catalog and a list. The labor pool is usually the easy part. Everyone usually has some teenagers, bored neighbors or someone who would like a little part-time work. It's not hard work, either — it entails placing stickers on envelopes, stuffing envelopes and filling orders.

You will need to invest some cash into self-advertising. While you don't need a glossy, full-color, 24-page catalog, you should consider a one- or two-color direct-mail piece that folds to fit in a regular envelope. (It's a lot cheaper to mail than a larger size.) Include photographs of your products (with food, photos sell better

We have tried mail order using frozen beef, and it's difficult in the Southwest, especially in the warm months. It requires very expensive special packaging, and either frozen gel packs or dry ice.

than drawings). Usually, it pays to have the photos professionally shot. Again, the graphic design can be done by that same college student or local print shop, but seek a good printer. Looking professional really counts in mail order.

The hardest part is finding a good list. You can locate a list broker through a company that does contract mailings (look up "Mailing" in the yellow pages), who will charge you so much per thousand names and addresses, depending upon the difficulty he has in targeting the audience you want. For instance, if you merely want to mail to a zip code area that you know is relatively upscale, then that will be fairly inexpensive to obtain. Instead, maybe you wish to mail to males, aged between 21 and 45, with an annual income of over $40,000, who participate in outdoor sports and have contributed money to an environmental organization in the last year. It can be done, but it will be a lot more expensive. Your mailings will be more effective, but you have to weigh the effectiveness against the expense.

When you start out, see if you can lay your hands on a free list that contains your target audience. If you or a good friend is a member of a special interest group such as *Californians for the Ferret*, it may be a good bet. Remember to always get permission first. It is illegal to use a list without permission.

Using the Internet to advertise your products can be great, as long as you are very specific about the areas you serve. You want to avoid fielding those endless inquiries from foreign countries that are out of your shipping zones. You can also take orders and process credit cards on the Internet. When we checked into the start-up costs, we couldn't justify the costs with our low volume, but, depending on the scope of your business, it might be worth it for you.

CATALOGS

If you get your product into an existing catalog, they do all the work. However, you only receive a portion of the sales price. Most catalogs retain 50 to 70 percent of the sales price. Granted, they handle the lists, the catalog, the shipping and all the customer-service details, but they also get a great portion of the cash. For that, they reach thousands more people than you can on your own, so you'll have a lot more volume. You'll have to weigh the two factors and see what is best for you.

The big catalogs are notoriously hard to get into. They have huge merchandising departments that receive and analyze hundreds of potential products per day. Even after you convince the merchandising person that your product will sell well, have a decent profit margin, and a low level of customer-service problems, it will be analyzed on a weekly

basis for its profit-per-square-inch performance. In other words, a product must contribute a certain profit for each square inch that it takes up in the catalog. Some excellent products may never make it in a catalog just because it takes too much text to explain it properly. The moment it falls below a pre-determined level, it is dropped. Yet, if you have a hot product in a good catalog, it can mean years of profitability.

It is sometimes advisable to get a sales representative when dealing with catalog companies. They are experienced in negotiating the best deal with the merchandising personnel (who can be ruthless), and with moving you to a different catalog if you are not performing well in a particular one. They charge a percentage of the sale.

Distribution and Trucking

When it comes to transportation, every situation is different. Retail distributors (who wholesale to stores) charge about a 35-percent markup. Restaurant distributors charge about 8 percent. Most other trucking firms charge by weight.

Don't be afraid to dicker over your price or percent with truckers or distributors. They are very supply-and-demand oriented. Being a small customer, you probably won't have the clout to push your weight around, but it doesn't hurt to ask.

With any kind of trucking be very specific:
- Frequency per week, day, month
- Pick up times
- Delivery times
- Who loads and unloads
- Who signs for pick-ups
- Who signs for delivery
- Pallet sizes
- Minimum weights
- Additional costs for unscheduled runs
- Other fees: pallet, lading (freight/cargo)

Marketing Your Product

Marketing involves two separate, but interrelated areas — sales and advertising. You will need both areas to work together to effectively market your product. It is ideal to have one person be the decision maker for all of marketing. I have seen a lot of large companies flounder simply because their sales and advertising departments were marching to a different drummer.

SALES BASICS

If you decide that restaurants, stores or distributors are the best avenue to sell your product, then you are going to have to make a sales call. If you have had no experience in sales, like most ranchers, here are the basics.

Make a client list that fits your size, marketing goals and so on. Call a potential client on the phone. You will probably get a secretary on the line. Tell him or her that you

PHOTO BY EDWIN REMSBERG

SELLING PRODUCT

are John Smith from John's Natural Beef Company and you are interested in getting your beef into their restaurant or store or catalog and ask to whom you should speak. Be very, very nice to the secretary or receptionist. A secretary or receptionist can be a huge ally or a huge enemy. Thank him or her profusely for the help. Make a note of his or her name, the contact's name, and get the right spellings. Ask for the contact by name after that. You may have to speak with three or four people to get the right one.

Before you go to your appointment, do a little homework. Visit the store or restaurant. Look at their customers. Look at what products they offer and how much space they are given. Find out how long they have been in business. Anything that you learn will help you in your discussion with your potential client.

Practice on an unlikely client. Go in like you expect to do well, but use it as an opportunity to learn how to make a call.

When you get to your appointment, you want to have the following items with you, and four or five sets of each — your brochure, business card, a price list with all items that are available and a proposal. The proposal should state exactly what items you want your client to carry and all pertinent information. This may include delivery information, ordering information, scheduling and sales support material availability.

Bring two sets of product samples. Do not charge them for their samples. The client will expect the samples to appear exactly as the product they will be selling or distributing, down to the last comma on the label. Make sure the samples are perfect. If you are going to sell a frozen product, make sure it is frozen hard. Bring the samples in a pristine ice chest. That one you take to the lake that smells like fish should stay home. Dress like a rancher, but a clean rancher.

Send a thank-you letter to the prospective client a few days later. Say that you will call in a few days to see how he or she liked your product. Then follow up promptly and you are off and running.

If the client is not interested in your product, don't hesitate to ask why. Ask if he or she knows someone who may be interested in what you have to offer. Tell them you respect their opinion. I have received a lot of useful advice and referrals this way. A few times I've gotten some very powerful people to call friends of theirs and set up appointments for me, merely because I told them that I would really appreciate their advice.

> Take multiple copies of your brochure, business card, price list and your proposal to every sales appointment; bring two perfect sets of product samples, and do not charge for them.

LOGO & SALES SUPPORT MATERIAL

You will need the following materials when you begin: a logo, stationery and a simple brochure. There are three things to remember:

- Keep it simple.
- Make sure the pieces reflect the taste of the people who will buy your product, not you.
- The quality of your materials directly reflects on the quality of your product.

In my 20-plus years in advertising, I've found that most people, including a lot of seemingly intelligent people, use this opportunity to feed their own egos. I cannot count the number of times that I have had a client insist that their company logo needs to be purple (or whatever) – because it is his wife's favorite color. Name your company something that appeals to your customer, use colors that will appeal to your customer, use language that they can understand. Get your own ego out of it. Your expertise is in beef production, not in design.

Spend time figuring out who wants your product and write it down. Take all this information and create an imaginary perfect customer. Revisit that perfect customer every time you need to make a decision about your sales support material.

Keep your look consistent; it will help people recognize you. Your brochure should be consistent with your label. Your label should be consistent with your business cards.

Now that you know who your target customer is, you can have your material designed. Call a community college with a graphic design department, or try a small printing company. They usually have an on-staff designer and they are very reasonable if you also allow them to print the job.

Do not have it done by a relative, or an old baby sitter, or even your spouse. Also, unless you have recently received a large inheritance, do not go to a professional graphic design company or advertising agency. These types of companies will charge you thousands of dollars more than you need to spend when you are starting out.

Your Logo. Don't rush your name and logo. You don't want to invest a lot of money and time into something only to find it's terribly wrong and you'll have to do it all over. Draw up a few of your favorites and put them up where you and, preferably, your target market can look and comment on them every day for about a week (a refrigerator, office cooler, bathroom mirror). After a while, you will see some definite winners emerging and some definite losers. It will make your decision easy.

First you need a name. Make sure that it is relatively short, and keep in mind your target customer. Alan Nation, editor of the Stockman Grass Farmer, believes that you should name it after yourself or your family. The most important aspect of your product is your credibility — and using your name

reinforces that belief. It gives you leverage when you sell your company to Ted Turner for billions of dollars. Ted will want to keep Fred Smith as a spokesperson on retainer with Fred's Family Beef for at least 10 years. That sounds like a very good reason to us.

Go with simple graphics. Consider a simple type treatment, perhaps an old woodcut or simple drawing. Leave the tricky symbols to professional graphic designers. Unless done extremely well they usually look dated in a few years. Moreover, logo design can be more costly than you think.

Make it one color. Multi-color anything just adds expense to your printing jobs and makes consistency harder to control. And it will not add to your sales. People expect a great deal of sophistication when they see a complex logo, they won't expect it of you. You just need to look professional and credible.

Brochures. You will probably need a small brochure. People want to know something about who they're buying from. If you keep it simple enough, and don't put in pricing (which can change often), you will be able to use your brochure for a lot of things. The most cost-effective size is 8½ x 11 inches, folded twice so that it fits in a number 10, business-sized envelope. Make it one color, but do include a photo of yourself, or the family, if they work in your business at all. It adds little to the cost and it helps people identify with you. Have the photo taken with a digital camera if possible, so that you can email the photos along with your copy when sending your brochures to a printer, as well as to the media when soliciting coverage.

Have a professional take photos. You probably know someone who has shot some good wedding photos who will trade for some beef. Also, take some extra shots: one of you alone, some with your whole family. Dress in work clothes and pay attention to what is in the background. A horse or a barn and rolling hills is better than your wife's Toyota. You can always use some for your company's holiday cards or send some to *Acres* magazine when they do that article on you being a fabulous success.

Tell a little about yourself in the brochure. The most important thing to talk about is what this product will do for the customer. Mention the health aspects, the food safety issues, and how your product is better for the land. Describe your humane treatment of animals, how your ranching practices benefit endangered and threatened species, or how your customer's purchasing of a local product eliminates petroleum use.

Use recycled paper when you print, and have the printer include the appropriate recycled symbol in the bottom corner. The folks who will pay more for a natural, organic or grass-fed product expect you to have environmentally sensitive stationery, too.

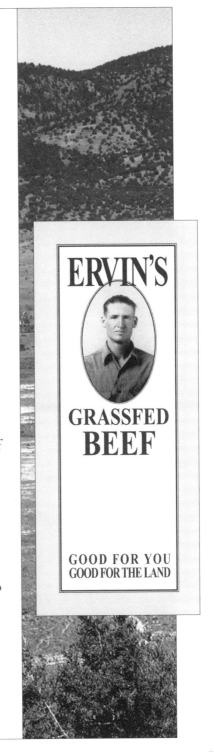

Advertising Basics

The two most important points to include in any advertising are:

- Customer Benefit: What's in it for the consumer? Does it taste better or is it better for the environment?
- Call to Action: After people have seen your ad, what next? Do you want them to call for more information, buy now, or look for you at the store? End every ad with a call to action.

Effective advertising can actually be done in a number of ways. Beyond paid advertising, consider using public relations strategies: having articles written about you in newspapers, magazines, radio and television; product sampling events; or speaking engagements. The most important thing to remember is: Do not spend any time or money promoting your product to people who are not predisposed to buying your product and who do not have an avenue to do so.

We know of one struggling beef co-op that actually provided free samples to a state fair, even though less than $1/10$ of 1 percent were potential customers, and even worse, less than $1/30$ of 1 percent had an avenue in which to buy their beef. It cost them thousands and thousands of dollars to reach a tiny percentage of their potential target customers.

Here is a good rule of thumb regarding advertising: When introducing yourself to a new market, your advertising should create a 15-percent increase in demand (compounded) with each showing, and plateau after about four showings. The percent varies depending on industry and maturity of market, but it is a good place to start.

Public Relations

You can obtain a lot of free PR, but it usually requires some effort on your part. Are you doing something interesting that could make a news story? If you have a story to tell, the press will probably write about it. Are you raising your beef differently than your neighbors? Are you fencing off areas for a threatened species? Are you providing internships for local kids?

Call the local papers and ask who covers environmental issues, agricultural issues or human interest. Then write a note to the appropriate person and include all the pertinent details. It doesn't have to be too fancy, but make sure it goes to the correct person. Include one of your brochures and the name and number of a contact person, in case they need more information or they want to send out a reporter or photographer. Hit all local TV, radio, newspapers and magazines. When you get a little larger, it will be helpful to make up a press kit. This will contain all the information in your brochure, plus a lot more specific information about yourself, your beliefs, and your operation. Also include any press clippings at the back.

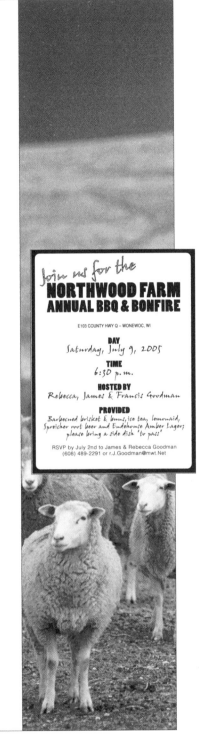

Another way to obtain free exposure is to offer yourself for speaking engagements.

Call local civic clubs if you have an interesting story to tell. Locate the special-interest clubs in your area that might be interested in what you have to say. Maybe it's a story about your efforts to restore health to the rangeland. Again, make sure that these are your target customers. Speaking at a soup kitchen shelter may be a wonderful thing to do, but those people are probably not going to have the discretionary income to purchase your product. Speaking to the local chapter of the Sierra Club, if you are speaking of your ranch's conservation efforts, is probably a better bet.

The same is true for product sampling. It works really well to distribute samples to a pre-qualified group. For instance, we give out product information and samples at our biggest client's yearly new-product fair. We give out jerky samples at farmers markets. We give our beef to a wildlife rehabilitation center's annual fund-raising dinner.

Paid advertising in newspapers, magazines, yellow pages, outdoor boards, radio and television are generally useless to the small beef producer. They are too expensive to cost-effectively reach your narrowly targeted customers. Do not even speak to the advertising salespeople who will contact you. They are armed with a lot of charts, graphs, demographics, psychographics, doublespeak, and gobbledygook. Remember: All advertising salespeople have their agendas. They will do anything to sell a $30 radio spot. That is all you need to know.

The kind of paid advertising that works well is narrow in focus. Match your advertising plan to your target market. Advertise in catalogs that sell your product, but not if you focus on farmers markets or sides of beef. Give away informational flyers in the stores that carry your products. Print up small table tents to place on tables in restaurants that sell your products. These are generally very effective and inexpensive.

Remember to stress the benefits to the consumer. Make it simple. Don't try to say too much in one ad. Make all type at least 12 points in size. Make headlines very short. Always include your logo and where to buy your product. Always include a "call to action." Tell them clearly what you want them to do: "Call 1-928-428-0033 and order today," or "stop by Tucson Cooperative's Cash-and-Carry Outlet and pick up some steaks today!"

The Internet is the hot advertising medium right now. Some producers find that websites — such as LocalHarvest.org and EatWild.com, which maintain directories of direct market farmers — provide good promotional channels. Local Harvest, for example, calls its nationwide directory of local food sources "the no. 1 informational resource for the 'buy local' movement and the top place on the Internet where people find information on direct marketing family

> The kind of paid advertising that works well is narrow in focus. Match your advertising plan to your target market. Advertise in catalogs that sell your product, but not if you focus on farmers markets or sides of beef.

SELLING PRODUCT

farms." You can register yourself for free, and their search engine will help people find you when they're looking for meat produced off the grid.

It may or may not work for you. We found that directory-type websites are an excellent resource for our customers to learn more about us, our company and our standards. Since we developed our own website, our telephone time spent with customers wanting to know if we treat our cattle humanely, or if we feed animal by-products, has been cut almost to nothing. However accepting online orders never worked for us. It is simply impossible in Arizona to ship product even overnight with specialized packaging, and have it arrive intact in the month of August. Even though we were specific about the geographic area that we serve, we continually had to field inquiries from far away spots like Japan. So we use the web as an educational support system for our clients.

Record Keeping

As a cattle rancher, you probably already have a bookkeeping system. It might be a simple manual system or a sophisticated computer program. Whatever it is, separate the books for your beef marketing company from your personal and ranch books. This will enable you to clearly define the performance of your new endeavor. I know that most ranchers just lump all their personal finances in with their ranch finances. Yet, it is important to at least separate your beef company on paper, or you will never be able to tell exactly how much money you generate.

These simple forms keep us organized:
- Master log-in form: Orders are numbered and logged in. Other forms and invoices pertaining to these orders share the same reference number. This keeps us from mixing up orders.
- Job order form: Contains all ordering information. After the order is paid, we file them by client so that we can refer to them later (*left*).
- A delivery receipt: We use this when we deliver to stores. It is signed and dated by the recipient in a space provided. With small stores, different people may log in deliveries on different days, so getting a signature is crucial.
- Invoice: The original job order form becomes an invoice after the order is delivered. We generate these on the computer and keep them in a separate file until the invoice is paid. We file them by client (*right*).

We also have started keeping records of sales by product and by month. We have found that there is a great deal of variance in sales over the year. For instance, sales tend to plummet during late December and early January. Sales tend to be the highest, especially for steaks, in the summer months. Keeping the numbers and charting them has helped us schedule our cattle more effectively.

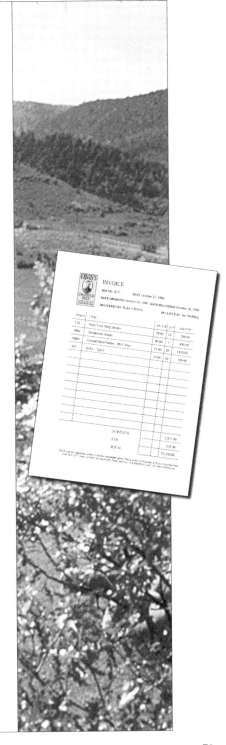

SELLING PRODUCT

79

growing profit

Many small cattle ranchers are suffering financially these days. With the increased costs of operating a ranch, the decreased returns of commodity beef, the additional scrutiny that faces public land ranchers and the pressure from many environmental groups, it's a wonder that anyone raises cattle at all.

Yet, through direct marketing there is a world of opportunity. Research shows that the organic and grass-fed markets are making huge incremental gains each year. Many people are looking for local products to feed their family. The increase in food safety issues such as BSE (bovine spongiform encephalopathy), or mad cow disease, brings even more opportunities for the small, local producer.

Our Vision of the Future for Small Beef Operations

Many family farms and ranches are simply too small to play the commodity game. Stan Parsons, of the Ranching for Profit School, figures you need a minimum of 1,000 head to be profitable. If you don't, you need to find a new game. Direct marketing is a good game.

Worldwide, the organic market is the fastest-growing segment of the food industry. We are just now beginning a nutritional revolution that will revive demand for grass-fed beef, lamb, chicken and dairy. This period is to family farming what the 1970s were to Silicone Valley, or what the 1940s were to Detroit.

If you have the marketing skills, or the desire to develop them, you will thrive in this demand-driven market segment. This is one of those periods in history when you want to have all your ducks in a row. Ride this wave up and have yourself positioned when the market matures in 15 to 20 years.

Developing Growth

As soon as you have your first client on board, you will be tempted to go out and try to bring on lots more. Since we are selling six head a month with no problems, won't 60 per month just be better? Won't that get the ranch out of our financial hole just that much quicker? Try to calm yourself down and be sensible. Grow slowly. Do not assume that now that you have the first client, the others will be easy. They're not.

Each client is unique and will keep you busy solving all the different problems. Remember, if you disappoint a client once and don't make that delivery, he or she will probably dump you. Very few restaurants, stores and distributors will forgive you. After all, they had to disappoint their customers too. They lost sales. They lost money, and it is your fault.

As long as you are centering on one type of business, small health food chains, for example, keep adding chains, one by one, making sure that you solve the problems one by one as they come up. Give each new acquisition, no matter how small, to your family of clients a minimum of a month or two to become familiar with your product and your company. Learn their way of doing things.

Say you decide to take on a client in a type of business that is different from anything you've handled before. You have three small chains of health food stores that are doing very nicely. You know the purchasing people now and they ask for you by name. Recently you made a presentation to a new distributor. He wants you. You want him. But take it slow.

Remember, you reinvented the wheel here. Every new type of business has its own set of challenges. Give a major new client six months to work the bugs out. We know that seems like a long time, but it is a lot better to have four happy customers than to take on 10 and lose nine because of problems.

Maximizing Your Performance

You may hear mention of beef "fitting in the box." That means your carcass is generally suited for mass-marketed beef, but it's hard to know what they want.

Each segment of the industry makes its money differently. The calf people make their money off cows that cycle back quickly. The stocker people make their money off fast growth on grass. The feedlot people make their money keeping their lot full. The packers make their money by slaughtering as many animals as they can.

So where does tenderness or marbling come into play? It usually doesn't mean too much if you're selling commodity beef. However, there are some exceptions. Bill Niman (*right*), founder of Niman Ranch, built a reputation for quality. For the rest of us, until the industry vertically integrates, there won't be much additional profit in creating a better product for the commodity markets.

With all that in mind, you can see that most of those cogs in the wheels of big industry don't apply to you. You will have to be your own research agent. There are a lot of folks like you out there doing different things. You will want to network with them and compare results.

What kind of cattle are the best for a grass-fed niche in Alabama? What is the point of diminishing returns with a grain-on-grass program in Utah? If you are lucky, you may find some research, but it's been our experience never to believe anything until you try it yourself.

There is a lot more good information out there than when we started. Most of the organizations and information listed in ***Resources*** (p. 88) are pretty new. With any luck and a lot of planning, you won't make all the mistakes we made. Despite the trials we went through, we are very happy with our choice to direct market our beef. We think you will be, too.

RICHARD AND PEGGY SECHRIST ON THEIR TEXAS RANCH — PHOTO BY PEGGY JONES

Factors that Impact Your Bottom Line

Written by Dan, Peggy & Richard Sechrist

What follows are some of the nitty-gritty details you need to consider in your profit equation. While you probably want to consider these options before launching a direct-marketing strategy, there is always opportunity to revisit these costs at any stage of the game.

Production costs. If you want to truly calculate your profit margin when direct marketing beef, you must include the full cost of production. You may even want to treat production costs as a separate "business" in your bookkeeping. Production costs are the total cost of the raw material needed to create your packaged product. It is essential to know if your gross profit covers the replacement value for the animals you are selling.

Processing costs. Processing costs for individual beef producers can vary a great deal and can take a big chunk out of your bottom line. The easiest way to compute and monitor processing costs is to calculate per head. The difference between your total cost and the total price you receive from the sale of each animal is your profit margin. The retail market price of beef is heavily influenced by the large beef packers who process several thousand head of cattle per day in their own facilities. This volume gives them a competitive edge by lowering their processing costs per head, and allowing them to set a low market price on beef. By contrast, individual beef producers may pay as much as 800 to 900 percent higher costs for processing and still need to price their beef within a competitive range. So managing your processing costs is very critical to your bottom line.

Market requirements. Who you are processing for is a related cost that requires careful management. When you decide to market your own beef, you may sell to three different markets:

- Distributors, who re-sell your beef to retailers
- Wholesale markets, such as retail food stores and restaurants
- Direct to consumers

The sales price structure for each of these segments is different. You receive the highest price when you sell direct to consumers. You receive a lower price for wholesale, and lower still for distributors. The requirements for how you cut and package your beef may differ among these market segments, too.

For example, the distributor may want each steak and roast "portion cut," meaning that each cut weighs exactly the same. Portion cutting adds additional cost to your processing fees while generating the lowest price. Wholesale customers may also make special requests that add to your costs. Selling direct to consumers may require you to use a USDA-approved label. You will need to discuss this with the licensed inspector at your processing plant. All these marketing options directly impact your profit margin. It pays to research and analyze your markets before you spend much money on your processing.

Carcass yields. It's important to calculate the percentage of each animal that returns to you as saleable beef after processing. That percentage can either help you achieve your desired profit margin — or wipe it out completely. There are industry averages, but there is so much variance that it behooves a producer who direct markets his own meat to calculate — in pounds — how much beef is available to sell after processing, then calculate what that available beef will return to see if the resulting profit margin is acceptable. Each animal is a bit unique in its capacity to finish.

Collecting data from each animal as it is processed — or averaging each group of animals processed — is vital to determine which slaughter weight leads to the highest yield of meat to sell.

Your yield from live weight to boxed beef is the yield you want to track. If you process 100 animals, all at 1,000 pounds live weight, your yield could vary more than you realize if you don't collect that data. If your yield of meat drops by as little as 3 to 5 percent, you can lose a large portion or even all of your profit. For example, a 5-percent yield deviation on 100 animals processed at 1,000 pounds live weight could reduce your profit margin by $20,000. Tracking this information as it occurs gives you a window of opportunity to strategize how to regain some profit before your product is sold.

Storage and obsolescence risk. There is substantial risk to creating a high number of different cuts to satisfy all the requests you may receive. You could butcher a carcass into 20 or more different cuts in pursuit of different customers. Yet, unless you have a guaranteed commitment for a special cut, you could easily find yourself with a stockpile of those cuts in frozen storage. The revenue that these cuts represent, along with their storage costs, could easily wipe out your profit margin.

A similar risk is to discount cuts that accumulate in storage. Discounting also will reduce your profit. Eight to nine of the most popular cuts give you the greatest flexibility to sell the whole carcass within a reasonable period of time.

Management skills. Managing the sale of several beef cuts as opposed to selling a live animal requires different management methods. You'll find it important to know exactly what your total cost is in each animal as well as knowing exactly what your gross profit is for each animal. Because small deviation in yields or accumulation of a few cuts can so dramatically impact your bottom line, you will want to track your return on each animal and be poised to make adjustments before you find yourself somewhere in the red. ■

resources

Agriculture Marketing Resource Center. A national information center for value-added agriculture. www.agmrc.org. Information on "natural," organic and direct marketing beef. www.agmrc.org/agmrc/commodity/livestock/beef/beef.htm.

Alternative Farming Systems Information Center (AFSIC). Provides free assistance and resources to farmers and agricultural professionals, including information on livestock production and marketing. (301) 504-6559; www.nal.usda.gov/afsic

ATTRA. National information service offers 200+ free publications on farming and marketing, many about livestock production and marketing. (800) 346-9140 / Spanish (800) 411-3222. http://attra.ncat.org/

Direct and Local Meat Marketing Project, University of Kentucky. Online resource for livestock producers includes budget spreadsheets and yield and pricing guides. www.uky.edu/ag/kymeat

Sustainable Agriculture Research and Education (SARE). SARE provides grants to researchers, agricultural educators and producers to study and spread information about sustainable agriculture, including direct marketing, via a nationwide grants program. (301) 504-5230; www.sare.org

Sustainable Agriculture Network (SAN). SAN delivers cutting-edge research results with books, bulletins and electronic resources for producers, educators and researchers. (301) 504-5236; www.sare.org

USDA Small Business Development Centers. Provides management assistance to current and prospective small business owners. 800-8-ask-sba; www.sba.gov/sbdc/

PUBLICATIONS

Adding Value to Beef Production. Assists those beginning a value-added agriculture business venture with tried-and-true methods. Iowa State University Extension. www.ciras.iastate.edu/beefmanual

Alternative Beef Marketing by ATTRA. Explores marketing alternatives for small-scale cattle ranchers who want to add value to their beef. www.attra.org/attra-pub/beefmark.html

Alternative Meat Marketing by ATTRA. Includes production and processing, direct marketing options, legal/regulatory considerations, organic certification and targeting ethnic markets. http://attra.ncat.org/attra-pub/altmeat.html

Building a Sustainable Business: A Guide to Developing a Business Plan for Farms and Rural Businesses. Transform farm-grown inspirations into profitable enterprises with sample worksheets for researching processing options, potential markets and financing. 280 pp. $17 to the Sustainable Agriculture Network, (301) 374-9696, www.sare.org/WebStore

How to Direct Market Meat – Is It An Option for You? by Anastasia Becker, Community Food Systems and Sustainable Agriculture, University of Missouri Outreach and Extension. http://aes.missouri.edu/swcenter/sustain

Direct Sales of Beef. Suggestions for selling beef directly to consumers. Nebraska Cooperative Extension. http://ianrpubs.unl.edu/beef/g1420.htm

The E Myth Revisited by Michael Gerber. Dispels the myths about starting your own business. 288 pp. $16. (866) 201-7601; www.powells.com

Energy-Efficient Grass-Based Meat and Veal Production and Marketing Manual. Center for Agricultural Development & Entrepreneurship, www.cadefarms.org/publications.htm

Grass Productivity by André Voisin. Maximizing productivity in grass and cattle operations from one of the earliest proponents. 370 pp. $30. www.Amazon.com

Holistic Resource Management by Allan Savory. Practical instruction in financial, biological and land planning. Case studies drawn from real-life situations lead the reader through the process. 590 pp. Prices vary. www.Amazon.com

Marketing Grass-fed Beef by the Kansas Rural Center. Marketing pamphlet with gross margin marketing worksheet. kansasruralcenter.org/publications/grassfedbeef.pdf

The Meat Buyers Guide by the North American Meat Processors Association. Meat identification manual, with more than 295 illustrated cuts, buying and ordering procedures, nutrition data, food safety and grading standards. 199 pp. $52, www.Amazon.com

The New Farmers' Market by Eric Gibson. Tips and trends from leading sellers to best display and sell product. 272 pp. $24.95. (301) 374-9696; www.sare.org/WebStore

Organic Livestock Workbook: A Guide to Sustainable and Allowed Practices by ATTRA. http://attra.ncat.org/attra-pub/PDF/livestockworkbook.pdf

Pasture Profits with Stocker Cattle by Allan Nation. How to improve profits with less financial risk. 224 pp. $28.50. Stockman Grass Farmer, (800) 748-9808; www.stockmangrassfarmer.com

Permaculture: A Designer's Manual by Bill Mollison. Philosophies of land use, soil, agricultural and livestock management, irrigation, and more. $75 (hard cover). www.Amazon.com

Salad Bar Beef by Joel Salatin. How to make a good profit with a small beef cattle operation. 368 pp. www.chelseagreen.com/1996/items/516

Shelter & Shade: Creating a Healthy and Profitable Environment for your Livestock with Trees by John & Bunny Mortimer. 160 pp. $20. The Stockman Grass Farmer, (800) 748-9808; www.stockmangrassfarmer.com

MAGAZINES

ACRES USA. A comprehensive guide to sustainable agriculture. (800) 355-5313; www.acresusa.com/magazines/magazine.htm

Small Farmer's Journal. Focuses on livestock breeds, organic farming and equipment. (800) 876-2893; www.smallfarmersjournal.com

Stockman Grass Farmer. Describes grazing technology and pasture management. (800) 748-9808; www.stockmangrassfarmer.com/sgf/

Small Farm Today. Preservation and promotion of small farming, rural living, community and sustainability. (800) 633-2535; www.smallfarmtoday.com